LEGENDS OF T

The Book of Saints and Friendly Beasts

Saint Francis of Assisi and Other Saints Who Loved Animals

Abbie Farwell Brown

Folklore and Mythology Archive
Kalevala Books, Chicago

"Stand at the crossroads and look; ask for the ancient paths, ask where the good way is, and walk in it, and you will find rest for your souls." — Jeremiah 6:16

The Book of Saints and Friendly Beasts: Saint Francis of Assisi and Other Saints Who Loved Animals

© 2010 Compass Rose Technologies, Inc. All rights reserved. No part of this book may be reproduced in any manner whatsoever without written permission, except in the case of brief quotations embodied in critical articles and reviews. Originally published as *The Book of Saints and Friendly Beasts* by Abbie Farwell Brown, Riverside Press, Cambridge, 1900. Cover illustration from *The Book of Fairy Poetry* by Dora Owen. Warwick Goble, illustrator. London: Longmans, Green, and Co., 1920. Title page illustration from www.karenswhimsy.com. Interior illustrations by Fanny Y. Cory.

Folklore and Mythology Archive and *Legends of the Christian Saints* series editor and designer: Joanne Asala.
www.CompassRose.com.

Published by
Kalevala Books
an imprint of
Compass Rose Technologies, Inc.
PO Box 409095
Chicago, IL 60640
www.CompassRose.com

Titles published by Kalevala Books are available at special quantity discounts to use as premiums and sales promotions or for academic use. For more information, please write to the Director of Special Sales, Compass Rose Technologies, Inc., PO Box 409095, Chicago, IL 60640 or contact us through our Web site, www.CompassRose.com.

ISBN: 978-1-880954-19-5

> I cannot tell how the truth may be; I say the tale as 'twas said to me.
> —Sir Walter Scott

In loving memory of a friendly beast.

Brother, hast thou never learned in holy writ, that with him who has led his life after God's will the wild beasts and wild birds are tame?

—Saint Guthlac of Crowland

Table of Contents

Introduction 1
Saint Bridget and the King's Wolf 3
Saint Gerasimus and the Lion 9
Saint Keneth of the Gulls 19
Saint Launomar's Cow 25
Saint Werburgh and Her Goose 31
The Ballad of Saint Athracta's Stags 39
Saint Kentigern and the Robin 45
Saint Blaise and His Beasts 51
Saint Cuthbert's Peace 55
The Ballad of Saint Felix 63
Saint Fronto's Camels 69
The Blind Singer Saint Hervé 75
Saint Comgall and the Mice 87
The Wonders of Saint Berach 91
Saint Prisca, The Child Martyr 97
The Fish Who Helped Saint Gudwall 103
The Ballad of Saint Giles and the Deer 107
The Wolf-Mother of Saint Ailbe 113
Saint Rigobert's Dinner 119
Saint Francis of Assisi 125
Calendar 133
Also Published by Kalevala Books 135

Introduction

In the old legends there may be things which some folk nowadays find it hard to believe. But surely the theme of each is true. It is not hard to see how gentle bodies who had no other friends should make comrades of the little folk in fur and fins and feathers. For, as St. Francis knew so well, all the creatures are our little brothers, ready to meet halfway those who will but try to understand. And this is a truth which every one today, even tho' he be no Saint, is waking up to learn. The happenings are set down quite as they read in the old books. Veritable histories, like those of St. Francis and St. Cuthbert, ask no addition of color to make them real. But sometimes, when a mere line of legend remained to hint of some dear Saint's relation with his friendly Beast, the story has been filled out in the way that seemed most likely to be true. For so alone could the old tale be made alive again. So all one's best is dressing old words new.

Saint Bridget and the King's Wolf

E very one has heard of Bridget, the little girl saint of Ireland. Her name is almost as well known as that of Saint Patrick, who drove all the snakes from the Island. Saint Bridget had long golden hair; and she was very beautiful. Many wonderful things happened to her that are written in famous books. But I suspect that you never heard what she did about the King's Wolf. It is a queer story.

This is how it happened. The King of Ireland had a tame wolf which some hunters had caught for him when it was a wee baby. And this wolf ran around as it pleased in the King's park near the palace, and had a very good time. But one morning he got over the high wall which surrounded the park, and strayed a long distance from home, which was a foolish thing to do. For in those days wild wolves were hated and feared by the people, whose cattle they often stole; and if a man could kill a wicked wolf he thought himself a very smart fellow indeed. Moreover, the King himself had offered a prize to any man who should bring him a dead wolf. For he wanted his kingdom to be a peaceful, happy one, where the children could play in the woods all day without fear of big eyes or big teeth.

Of course you can guess what happened to the King's wolf? A big, silly country fellow was going along with his bow and arrows, when he saw a great brown beast leap over a hedge and dash into the meadow beyond. It was only the King's wolf running away from home and feeling very frisky because it was the first time that he had done such a thing. But the country fellow did not know all that.

"Aha!" he said to himself. "I'll soon have you, my fine wolf; and the King will give me a gold piece that will buy me a hat and a new suit of clothes for the holidays." And without stopping to think about it or to look closely at the wolf who had the King's mark upon his ear, the fellow shot his arrow straight as a string. The King's wolf gave one great leap into the air and then fell dead on the grass, poor fellow.

The countryman was much pleased. He dragged his prize straight up to the King's palace and thumped on the gate.

"Open!" he cried. "Open to the valiant hunter who has shot a wolf for the King. Open, that I may go in to receive the reward."

So, very respectfully, they bade him enter; and the Lord Chamberlain escorted him before the King himself who sat on a great red-velvet throne in the Hall. In came the fellow, dragging after him by the tail the limp body of the King's wolf.

"What have we here?" growled the King, as the Lord Chamberlain made a low bow and pointed with his staff to the stranger. The King had a bad temper and did not like to receive callers in the morning. But the silly countryman was too vain of his great deed to notice the King's disagreeable frown.

"You have here a wolf, Sire," he said proudly. "I have shot for you a wolf, and I come to claim the promised reward."

But at this unlucky moment the King started up with an angry cry. He had noticed his mark on the wolf's right ear.

"Ho! Seize the villain!" he shouted to his soldiers. "He has slain my tame wolf; he has shot my pet! Away with him to prison; and to-morrow he dies."

It was useless for the poor man to scream and cry and try to explain that it was all a mistake. The King was furious. His wolf was killed, and the murderer must die.

In those days this was the way kings punished men who displeased them in any way. There were no delays; things happened very quickly. So they dragged the poor fellow off to a dark, damp dungeon and left him there howling and tearing his hair, wishing that wolves had never been saved from the flood by Noah and his Ark.

Now not far from this place little Saint Bridget lived. When she chose the beautiful spot for her home there were no houses near, only a great oak-tree, under which she built her little hut. It had but one room and the roof was covered with grass and straw. It seemed almost like a doll's playhouse, it was so small; and Bridget herself was like a big, golden-haired wax doll, — the prettiest doll you ever saw.

She was so beautiful and so good that people wanted to live near her, where they could see her sweet face often and hear her voice. When they found where she had built her cell, men came flocking from all the country round about with their wives and children and

Saint Bridget and the King's Wolf

their household goods, their cows and pigs and chickens; and camping on the green grass under the great oak-tree they said, "We will live here, too, where Saint Bridget is."

So house after house was built, and a village grew up about her little cell; and for a name it had Kildare, which in Irish means "Cell of the Oak." Soon Kildare became so fashionable that even the King must have a palace and a park there. And it was in this park that the King's wolf had been killed.

Now Bridget knew the man who had shot the wolf, and when she heard into what terrible trouble he had fallen she was very sorry, for she was a kind-hearted little girl. She knew he was a silly fellow to shoot the tame wolf; but still it was all a mistake, and she thought he ought not to be punished so severely. She wished that she could do something to help him, to save him if possible. But this seemed difficult, for she knew what a bad temper the King had; and she also knew how proud he had been of that wolf who was the only tame one in all the land.

Bridget called for her coachman with her chariot and pair of white horses, and started for the King's palace, wondering what she should do to satisfy the King and make him release the man who had meant to do no harm.

But lo and behold! as the horses galloped along over the Irish bogs of peat, Saint Bridget saw a great white shape racing towards her. At first she thought it was a dog. But no, no dog was as large as that. She soon saw that it was a wolf, with big eyes and with a red tongue lolling out of his mouth. At last he overtook the frightened horses, and with a flying leap came plump into the chariot where Bridget sat, and crouched at her feet, quietly as a dog would. He was no tame wolf, but a wild one, who had never before felt a human being's hand upon him. Yet he let Bridget pat and stroke him, and say nice things into his great ear. And he kept perfectly still by her side until the chariot rumbled up to the gate of the palace.

Then Bridget held out her hand and called to him; and the great white beast followed her quietly through the gate and up the stair and down the long hall, until they stood before the red-velvet throne, where the King sat looking stern and sulky.

They must have been a strange-looking pair, the little maiden in her green gown with her golden hair falling like a shower down to her knees; and the huge white wolf standing up almost as tall as she, his yellow eyes glaring fiercely about, and his red tongue panting. Bridget laid her hand gently on the beast's head which was close to her shoulder, and bowed to the King. The King only sat and stared, he was so surprised at the sight; but Bridget took that as a permission to speak.

"You have lost your tame wolf, O King," she said. "But I have brought you a better. There is no other tame wolf in all the land, now yours is dead. But look at this one! There is no white wolf to be found anywhere, and he is both tame and white. I have tamed him, my King. I, a little maiden, have tamed him so that he is gentle as you see. Look, I can pull his big ears and he will not snarl. Look, I can put my little hand into his great red mouth, and he will not bite. Sire, I give him to you. Spare me then the life of the poor, silly man who unwittingly killed your beast. Give his stupid life to me in exchange for this dear, amiable wolf," and she smiled pleadingly.

The King sat staring first at the great white beast, wonderfully pleased with the look of him, then at the beautiful maiden whose blue eyes looked so wistfully at him. And he was wonderfully pleased with the look of them, too. Then he bade her tell him the whole story, how she had come by the creature, and when, and where. Now when she had finished he first whistled in surprise, then he laughed. That was a good sign. — he was wonderfully pleased with Saint Bridget's story, also. It was so strange a thing for the King to laugh in the morning that the Chamberlain nearly fainted from surprise; and Bridget felt sure that she had won her prayer. Never had the King been seen in such a good humor. For he was a vain man, and it pleased him mightily to think of owning all for himself this huge beast, whose like was not in all the land, and whose story was so marvelous.

And when Bridget looked at him so beseechingly, he could not refuse those sweet blue eyes the request which they made, for fear of seeing them fill with tears. So, as Bridget begged, he pardoned the countryman, and gave his life to Bridget, ordering his soldiers to set him free from prison. Then when she had thanked the King very sweetly, she bade the wolf lie down beside the red-velvet throne, and thenceforth be faithful and kind to his new master. And with one last

Saint Bridget and the King's Wolf

ST. BRIDGET & THE KING'S WOLF

pat upon his shaggy head, she left the wolf and hurried out to take away the silly countryman in her chariot, before the King should have time to change his mind.

The man was very happy and grateful. But she gave him a stern lecture on the way home, advising him not to be so hasty and so wasty next time.

"Sirrah Stupid," she said as she set him down by his cottage gate, "better not kill at all than take the lives of poor tame creatures. I have saved your life this once, but next time you will have to suffer. Remember, it is better that two wicked wolves escape than that one kind beast be killed. We cannot afford to lose our friendly beasts, Master Stupid. We can better afford to lose a blundering fellow like you." And she drove away to her cell under the oak, leaving the silly man to think over what she had said, and to feel much ashamed.

But the King's new wolf lived happily ever after in the palace park; and Bridget came often to see him, so that he had no time to grow homesick or lonesome.

Saint Gerasimus and the Lion

One fine morning Saint Gerasimus was walking briskly along the bank of the River Jordan. By his side plodded a little donkey bearing on his back an earthen jar; for they had been down to the river together to get water, and were taking it back to the monastery on the hill for the monks to drink at their noonday meal.

Gerasimus was singing merrily, touching the stupid little donkey now and then with a twig of olive leaves to keep him from going to sleep. This was in the far East, in the Holy Land, so the sky was very blue and the ground smelled hot. Birds were singing around them in the trees and overhead, all kinds of strange and beautiful birds. But suddenly Gerasimus heard a sound unlike any bird he had ever known; a sound which was not a bird's song at all, unless some newly invented kind had a bass voice which ended in a howl. The little donkey stopped suddenly, and bracing his fore legs and cocking forward his long, flappy ears, looked afraid and foolish. Gerasimus stopped too. But he was so wise a man that he could not look foolish. And he was too good a man to be afraid of anything. Still, he was a little surprised.

"Dear me," he said aloud, "how very strange that sounded. What do you suppose it was?" Now there was no one else anywhere near, so he must have been talking to himself. For he could never have expected that donkey to know anything about it. But the donkey thought he was being spoken to, so he wagged his head, and said, "He-haw!" which was a very silly answer indeed, and did not help Gerasimus at all.

He seized the donkey by the halter and waited to see what would happen. He peered up and down and around and about, but there was nothing to be seen except the shining river, the yellow sand, a clump of bushes beside the road, and the spire of the monastery peeping over the top of the hill beyond. He was about to start the donkey once more on his climb towards home, when that sound came again; and this time he noticed that it was a sad sound, a sort of whining growl ending in a sob. It sounded nearer than before, and seemed to come from the clump of bushes. Gerasimus and the donkey turned their heads quickly in that direction, and the donkey trembled all over, he was so frightened. But his master only said, "It must be a Lion!"

And sure enough: he had hardly spoken the word when out of the bushes came poking the great head and yellow eyes of a lion. He was looking straight at Gerasimus. Then, giving that cry again, he bounded out and strode towards the good man, who was holding the donkey tight to keep him from running away. He was the biggest kind of a lion, much bigger than the donkey, and his mane was long and thick, and his tail had a yellow brush on the end as large as a window mop. But as he came Gerasimus noticed that he limped as if he were lame. At once the Saint was filled with pity, for he could not bear to see any creature suffer. And without any thought of fear, he went forward to meet the lion. Instead of pouncing upon him fiercely, or snarling, or making ready to eat him up, the lion crouched whining at his feet

"Poor fellow," said Gerasimus, "what hurts you and makes you lame, brother Lion?"

The lion shook his yellow mane and roared. But his eyes were not fierce; they were only full of pain as they looked up into those of Gerasimus asking for help. And then he held up his right fore paw and shook it to show that this was where the trouble lay. Gerasimus looked at him kindly.

"Lie down, sir," he said just as one would speak to a big yellow dog. And obediently the lion charged. Then the good man bent over him, and taking the great paw in his hand examined it carefully. In the soft cushion of the paw a long pointed thorn was piercing so deeply that he could hardly find the end. No wonder the poor lion had roared with pain! Gerasimus pulled out the thorn as gently as he could, and though it must have hurt the lion badly he did not make a sound, but lay still as he had been told. And when the thorn was taken out the lion licked Gerasimus' hand, and looked up in his face as if he would say, "Thank you, kind man. I shall not forget."

Now when the Saint had finished this good deed he went back to his donkey and started on towards the monastery. But hearing the soft pad of steps behind him he turned and saw that the great yellow lion was following close at his heels. At first he was somewhat embarrassed, for he did not know how the other monks would receive this big stranger. But it did not seem polite or kind to drive him away, especially as he was still somewhat lame. So Gerasimus took up his switch of olive leaves and drove the donkey on without a word, thinking that perhaps the lion would grow tired and drop behind. But when he glanced over his shoulder he still saw the yellow head close at his elbow; and sometimes he felt the hot, rough tongue licking his hand that hung at his side.

So they climbed the hill to the monastery. Some one had seen Gerasimus coming with this strange attendant at his heels, and the windows and doors were crowded with monks, their mouths and eyes wide open with astonishment, peering over one another's shoulders. From every corner of the monastery they had run to see the sight; but they were all on tiptoe to run back again twice as quickly if the lion should roar or lash his tail. Now although Gerasimus knew that the house was full of staring eyes expecting every minute to see him eaten up, he did not hurry or worry at all. Leisurely he unloaded the water-jar and put the donkey in his stable, the lion following him everywhere he went. When all was finished he turned to bid the beast good-by. But instead of taking the hint and departing as he was expected to, the lion crouched at Gerasimus' feet and licked his sandals; and then he looked up in the Saint's face and pawed at his coarse gown pleadingly, as if he said, "Good man, I love you because you took the thorn out of my foot. Let me stay with you always to be your watch-dog." And Gerasimus understood.

"Well, if you wish to stay I am willing, so long as you are good," he said, and the lion leaped up and roared with joy so loudly that all the monks who were watching tumbled over one another and ran away to their cells in a terrible fright, locking the doors behind them.

Gerasimus carried the water-jar into the empty kitchen, and the lion followed. After sniffing about the place to get acquainted, just as a kitten does in its new home, the lion lay down in front of the fire and curled his head up on his paws, like the great big cat he was. And so after a long sigh he went to sleep. Then Gerasimus had a chance to tell the other monks all about it. At first they were timid and would not hear of keeping such a dangerous pet. But when they had all tiptoed down to the kitchen behind Gerasimus and had seen the big kitten asleep there so peacefully they were not quite so much afraid.

"I'll tell you what we will do," said the Abbot. "If Brother Gerasimus can make his friend eat porridge and herbs like the rest of us we will let him join our number. He might be very useful, — as well as ornamental,— in keeping away burglars and mice. But we cannot have any flesh-eating creature among us. Some of us are too fat and tempting, I fear," and he glanced at several of the roundest monks, who shuddered in their tight gowns. But the Abbot himself was the fattest of them all, and he spoke with feeling.

So it was decided. Gerasimus let the lion sleep a good long nap, to put him in a fine humor. But when it came time for supper he mixed a bowl of porridge and milk and filled a big wooden platter with boiled greens. Then taking one dish in each hand he went up to the lion and set them in front of his nose.

"Leo, Leo, Leo!" he called coaxingly, just as a little girl would call "Kitty, Kitty, Kitty!" to her pet. The lion lifted up his head and purred, like a small furnace, for he recognized his friend's voice. But when he smelled the dishes of food he sniffed and made a horrid face, wrinkling up his nose and saying "Ugh!" He did not like the stuff at all. But Gerasimus patted him on the head and said, "You had better eat it, Leo; it is all I have myself. Share and share alike, brother."

The lion looked at him earnestly, and then dipped his nose into the porridge with a grunt. He ate it all, and found it not so very bad. So next he tried the greens. They were a poor dessert, he thought; but since he saw that Gerasimus wanted him to eat them he finished the dish, and then lay down on the hearth feeling very tired.

Gerasimus was delighted, for he had grown fond of the lion and wanted to keep him. So he hurried back to the dining hall and showed the empty dishes to the Abbot. That settled the lion's fate. Thenceforth he became a member of the monastery. He ate with the other monks in the great hall, having his own private trencher and bowl beside Gerasimus. And he grew to like the mild fare of the good brothers, — at least he never sought for anything different. He slept outside the door of his master's cell and guarded the monastery like a faithful watch-dog. The monks grew fond of him and petted him so that he lived a happy life on the hill, with never a wish to go back to the desert with its thorns.

II.

Wherever Gerasimus went the lion went also. Best of all, Leo enjoyed their daily duty of drawing water from the river. For that meant a long walk in the open air, and a frolic on the bank of the Jordan. One day they had gone as usual, Gerasimus, the lion, and the stupid donkey who was carrying the filled jar on his back. They were jogging comfortably home, when a poor man came running out of a tiny hut near the river, who begged Gerasimus to come with him and try to cure his sick baby. Of course the good man willingly agreed; this was one of the errands which he loved best to do.

"Stay, brother," he commanded Leo, who wanted to go with him, "stay and watch the foolish donkey." And he went with the man, feeling sure that the lion would be faithful. Now Leo meant to do his duty, but it was a hot and sleepy day, and he was very tired. He lay down beside the donkey and kept one eye upon him, closing the other one just for a minute. But this is a dangerous thing to do. Before he knew it, the other eye began to wink; and the next moment Leo was sound asleep, snoring with his head on his paws. Then it was that the silly donkey began to grow restless. He saw a patch of grass just beyond that looked tempting, and he moved over to it. Then he saw a greener spot beyond that, and then another still farther beyond that, till he had taken his silly self a long way off. And just then there came along on his way from Dan to Beersheba, a thief of a Camel Driver, with a band of horses and asses. He saw the donkey grazing there with no one near, and he said to himself, —

"Aha! A fine little donkey. I will add him to my caravan and no one will be the wiser." And seizing Silly by the halter, he first cut away the water-jar, and then rode off with him as fast as he could gallop.

Now the sound of pattering feet wakened Leo. He jumped up with a roar just in time to see the Camel Driver's face as he glanced back from the top of the next hill. Leo ran wildly about sniffing for the donkey; but when he found that he had really disappeared, he knew the Camel Driver must have stolen him. He was terribly angry. He stood by the water-jar and roared and lashed his tail, gnashing his jaws as he remembered the thief's wicked face.

Now in the midst of his rage out came Gerasimus. He found Leo roaring and foaming at the mouth, his red-rimmed eyes looking very fierce. And the donkey was gone — only the water-jar lay spilling on the ground. Then Gerasimus made a great mistake. He thought that poor Leo had grown tired of being a vegetarian, of living upon porridge and greens, and had tried fresh donkey-meat for a change.

"Oh, you wicked lion!" he cried, "you have eaten poor Silly. What shall I do to punish you?" Then Leo roared louder than ever with shame and sorrow. But he could not speak to tell how it had happened. The Saint was very sad. Tears stood in his kind eyes. "You will have to be donkey now," he said; "you will have to do his part of the work since he is now a part of you. Come, stand up and let me fasten the water-jar upon your back." He spoke sternly and even switched Leo with his olive stick. Leo had never been treated like this. He was the King of Beasts, and it was shame for a King to do donkey's work. His eyes flashed, and he had half a mind to refuse and to run away. Then he looked at the good man and remembered how he had taken out that cruel thorn. So he hung his head and stood still to be harnessed in the donkey's place.

Slowly and painfully Leo carried the water-jar up the hill. But worse than all it was to feel that his dear master was angry with him. Gerasimus told the story to the other monks, and they were even more angry than he had been, for they did not love Leo so well. They all agreed that Leo must be punished; so they treated him exactly as if he were a mean, silly donkey. They gave him only oats and water to eat, and made him do all Silly's work. They would no longer let him sleep outside his master's door, but they tied him in a lonesome stall in the stable. And now he could not go to walk with Gerasimus free and happy as the King of Beasts should be. For he went only in harness, with never a kind word from his master's lips.

It was a sad time for Leo. He was growing thinner and thinner. His mane was rough and tangled because he had no heart to keep it smooth. And there were several white hairs in his beautiful whiskers. He was fast becoming melancholy; and the most pitiful beast in all

Saint Gerasimus and the Lion

the world is a melancholy lion. He had been hoping that something would happen to show that it was all a mistake; but it seemed as though the world was against him, and truth was dead.

It was a sad time for Gerasimus, too; for he still loved Leo, though he knew the lion must be punished for the dreadful deed which he was believed to have done. One day he had to go some distance to a neighboring town to buy provisions. As usual, he took Leo with him to bring back the burden, but they did not speak all the way. Gerasimus had done the errands which he had come to do, and was fastening the baskets on each side of the lion's back. A group of children were standing around watching the queer sight, — a lion burdened like a donkey! And they laughed and pointed their fingers at him, making fun of poor Leo.

But suddenly the lion growled and began to lash his tail, quivering like a cat ready to spring on a mouse. The children screamed and ran away, thinking that he was angry with them for teasing him. But it was not that. A train of camels was passing at the moment, and Leo had seen at their head a mean, wicked face which he remembered. And as the last of the caravan went by, Leo caught sight of Silly himself, the missing donkey of the monastery. At the sound of Leo's growl, Silly pricked up his ears and stood on his fore legs, which is not a graceful position for a donkey. Then the Camel Driver came running up to see what was the matter with his stolen donkey. But when he came face to face with Leo, whose yellow eyes were glaring terribly, the thief trembled and turned pale. For he remembered the dreadful roar which had followed him that day as he galloped away across the sand holding Silly's halter. The poor donkey was quivering with fear, thinking that this time he was surely going to be eaten piecemeal. But after all this trouble on Silly's account, the very idea of tasting donkey made Leo sick. He only wanted to show Gerasimus what a mistake had been made.

All this time Gerasimus had been wondering what the lion's strange behavior meant. But when he saw Leo seize the donkey's bridle, he began to suspect the truth. He ran up and examined the donkey carefully. Then Leo looked up in his face and growled softly, as if to say: —

"Here is your old donkey, safe and sound. You see I didn't eat him after all. That is the real thief," and turning to the Camel Driver, he showed his teeth and looked so fierce that the man hid behind a camel, crying, "Take away the lion! Kill the wicked lion!" But Gerasimus seized Silly by the bridle.

"This is my beast," he said, "and I shall lead him home with me. You stole him, Thief, and my noble lion has found you out," and he laid his hand tenderly on Leo's head.

"He is mine, you shall not have him!" cried the Camel Driver, dodging out from behind the camel, and trying to drag the donkey away from Gerasimus. But with a dreadful roar, Leo sprang upon him, and with his great paw knocked him down and sat upon his stomach.

"Do not hurt him, Leo," said Gerasimus gently. But to the Camel Driver he was very stern. "Look out, Sir Thief," he said, "how you steal again the donkey of an honest man. Even the yellow beasts of the desert know better than that, and will make you ashamed. Be thankful that you escape so easily."

Then he took the baskets from Leo's back and bound them upon Silly, who was glad to receive them once more from his own master's hands. For the Camel Driver had been cruel to him and had often beaten him. So he resolved never again to stray away as he had done that unlucky time. And when they were all ready to start, Gerasimus called Leo, and he got up from the chest of the Camel Driver, where he had been sitting all this time, washing his face with his paws and smiling.

"My poor old Leo!" said Gerasimus, with tears in his eyes. "I have made you suffer cruelly for a crime of which you were not guilty. But I will make it up to you."

Then happily the three set out for home, and all the way Gerasimus kept his arm about the neck of his lion, who was wild with joy because he and his dear master were friends once more, and the dreadful mistake was discovered.

They had a joyful reception at the monastery on the hill. Of course every one was glad to see poor Silly again; but best of all it was to know that their dear old lion was not a wicked murderer. They petted him and gave him so many good things to eat that he almost burst with fatness. They made him a soft bed, and all the monks took turns in scratching his chin for ten minutes at a time, which was what Leo loved better than anything else in the world.

And so he dwelt happily with the good monks, one of the most honored brothers of the monastery. Always together he and Gerasimus lived and slept and ate and took their walks. And at last after many, many years, they grew old together, and very tired and sleepy. So one night Gerasimus, who had become an Abbot, the head of the monastery, lay gently down to rest, and never woke up in the morning. But the great lion loved him so that when they laid Saint Gerasimus to sleep under a beautiful plane-tree in the garden, Leo lay down upon the mound moaning and grieving, and would not move. So his faithful heart broke that day, and he, too, slept forever by his dear master's side.

But this was not a sad thing that happened. For think how dreadful the days would have been for Leo without Gerasimus. And think how sad a life Gerasimus would have spent if Leo had left him first. Oh, no; it was not sad, but very, very beautiful that the dear Saint and his friendly beast could be happy together all the day, and when the long night came they could sleep together side by side in the garden.

Saint Keneth of the Gulls

Once upon a time, more than a thousand years ago, a great white seagull was circling above the waves which roll between South England and Wales. He was pretending that he was doing this just for fun; and he seemed very lazy and dozy as he poised and floated without much trouble to move his wings. But really he was looking for a dinner, though he did not want any one to suspect it. And he hoped that some unwary fish would swim up near the surface of the water within diving reach of his great claws. His keen gray eyes were open all the while unsleepily, and not much that was going on down below on the water escaped his notice.

Suddenly his eye caught sight of a little black speck on the waves. "Aha!" he said to himself, "I think I see my dinner!" and with a great swoop down he pounced. You could hardly think how anything which looked so lazy and quiet could dart so like a flash of lightning. But a gull is an air-ship that can sink whenever it chooses. And when he gives a fish a sudden invitation to step in for dinner, the fish is hardly able to refuse.

But this was no fish which the hungry gull had spied. Before he reached the water he saw his mistake, and wheeling swiftly as only a gull can, he flapped back again into the air, uttering a screech of surprise.

"Cree-e-e!" he cried. "'Tis no scaly water-fish such as I like to eat. 'Tis one of those smooth land-fishes with yellow seaweed growing on its head. What is it doing here? I must see to this. Cree-e-e!"

No wonder the great bird circled and swooped curiously over the wicker basket which was floating on the waves. For on a piece of purple cloth lay a tiny pink-and-white baby, sound asleep, his yellow hair curling about the dimpled face, and one thumb thrust into the round red mouth.

"Well, well!" said the sea-gull to himself when he had examined the strange floating thing all he wished. "I must go and tell the others about this. Something must be done. There is a storm brewing, and this boat will not bear much rough weather. This little land-fish

SAINT KENETH OF THE GULLS

cannot swim. We must take care of him. Cree-e-e!" So off he flapped, and as he went he gave the family cry to call the gulls about him, wherever they might be.

Soon they came, circling carelessly, swooping sulkily, floating

Saint Keneth of the Gulls

happily, darting eagerly, according to their various dispositions; and as they came they gave the Gull cry. "Cree-e-e!" said they, "what is the matter?" "Follow me," said the White Gull to the great fleet of gray-winged air-ships. "Follow me, and you shall see," (which is Gull poetry).

Then he led the flock over the spot where the wicker cradle tossed on the growing waves. "Lo," said he, "a land-fish in danger of being drowned among the Scaly Ones. Let us save it. See how pink it is. Its eyes are a piece of the sky, and its voice is not unlike ours — listen!"

For by this time the baby had wakened, and feeling cold and hungry and wet with the dashing spray, opened his pink mouth, and began to cry lustily. "E-e-e-e-e!" wailed the baby; and as the White Gull had said, that sounds very like the chief word of the Gull tongue.

"Poor little thing!" said all the mother gulls in chorus. "He talks our language, he must be saved. Come, brothers and sisters, and use your beaks and talons before the clumsy nest in which he lies is sunk beneath the waves. Cree-e-e, little one, cree-e-e! We will save you."

Now, I don't know what cree-e-e means in Gull. But the baby must have understood. For he stopped crying instantly, and looked up laughing at the white wings which fanned his face and the kind gray eyes which peered into his own blue ones.

So the strong gulls seized the corners of the purple cloth on which the baby lay, some with their claws, some with their hooked beaks. And at a signal from the White Gull they fluttered up and away, bearing the baby over the waves as if he were in a little hammock. The White Gull flew on before and guided them to land, — a high shelf which hung over the sea roaring on the rocks below, the nicest kind of a gull home. And here they laid the baby down, and sat about wondering what they must do next. But the baby cried.

"We must build him a nest," said the White Gull. "These rocks are too hard and too sharp for a little land-fish. I know how they sleep in their home nests, for I have seen."

Now the gulls lay their eggs on the bare rocks, and think these quite soft enough for the young gull babies. But they all agreed that this would never do for the little stranger. So they pulled the downy feathers from their breasts till they had a great pile; and of this they made the softest bed in which they laid the baby. And he slept.

This is how little Saint Keneth was saved from the waves by the kind sea-gulls. And it goes to show that birds are sometimes kinder than human folk. For Keneth was the Welsh Prince's little son. But no one loved him, and his cruel mother had put him into the wicker basket and set him afloat on the waves, not caring what became of him nor hoping to see him again. But this in after years she did, when Keneth was become a great and famous Saint whom all, even the Prince and Princess, honored. She did not know him then because she believed that he was dead. How proud she would have been if she could have called him "Son!" But that was many years later.

Now when the gulls had made Keneth this comfortable nest, they next wondered what they should do to get him food. But the White Gull had an idea. He flew away over the land and was gone for some time. When at last he returned he had with him a kind forest doe, — a yellow mother Deer who had left her little ones, at the White Gull's request, to come and feed the stranger baby. So Keneth found a new mother who loved him far better than his own had done, — a new mother who came every morning and every night and fed him with her milk. And he grew strong and fat and hearty, the happy baby in his nest upon the rocks, where his friends, the sea-gulls, watched over him, and the mother Deer fed and cared for him, and washed him clean with her warm crash-towel tongue.

Now when Keneth had lived in the seagulls' home for some months, one day the flock of guardian gulls left him while they went upon a fishing trip. The mother Deer had not yet come with his breakfast, but was at home with her own little ones, so that for the first time Keneth was quite alone. He did not know this, but was sleeping peacefully on his purple quilt, when a strange face came peering over the edge of the rocks. It was a Shepherd from the nearest village who had clambered up to seek gulls' eggs for his breakfast. But his eyes bulged out of his head, and he nearly fell over backward into the sea with surprise when he saw Keneth lying in his nest of feathers.

"The Saints preserve us!" he cried, "what is this?" But when he had climbed nearer and saw what it really was, he was delighted with the treasure which he had found. "A beautiful little baby!" he ex-

Saint Keneth of the Gulls

claimed. "I will take him home to my wife, who has no child of her own." And forthwith he took up Keneth, wrapped in the purple cloth, and started down over the rocks towards his home.

But Keneth wakened at the stranger's touch and began to wail. He had no mind to go with the Shepherd; he wanted to stay where he was. So as they went he screamed at the top of his lungs, hoping some of his friends would come. And the mother Deer, who was on her way thither, heard his voice. She came running in a fright, but she could do nothing to protect him, being a gentle, weaponless creature. However, she followed anxiously to see what would happen to her darling. So they went down the rocks, Keneth and the Shepherd, with the Deer close behind. And all the way Keneth shrieked loudly, "E-e-e-e!"

Now at last a messenger breeze carried the baby voice out over the water of the Bristol Channel where the gulls were fishing.

"What is that?" they said, stopping their work to listen. "Is it not our little land-fish calling us in Gull? He is in trouble or danger. Brothers, to the rescue! Cre-e-e-e!"

So the flock of gulls left their fishing and swooped back to the rock where they had left the baby. Dreadful! The nest was empty. They flapped their wide wings and screamed with fear, "What shall we do?"

But just then up the rocky hill came panting the mother Deer. Her glossy hide was warm and wet, and her tongue lolled out with weariness, she had run so fast.

"He is down there," she panted. "The Shepherd has carried him to his hut and laid him in a nest such as human-folk make. The Shepherd's wife loves him and would keep him there, but he is unhappy and cries for us. You must bring him back."

"We will, we will!" screamed the gulls in chorus. "Guide us to the place, mother Deer." And without another word they rose on their great, strong wings, and followed where she led. Back down the hill she took the path, over the moor and up the lane to a little white cottage under the rosebushes. "Here is the place," said the Deer, and she paused.

But the flock of gulls with a great whirring and rustling and screaming swooped in at the little low door, straight up to the cradle where Keneth lay crying "E-e-e-e!" as if his heart would break.

The Shepherd's wife was sitting by the cradle saying, "Hush!" and "Bye-lo!" and other silly things that Keneth did not understand. But when she heard the rushing of the gulls' wings, she gave a scream and started for the door.

"Cree-e-e!" cried the gulls fiercely. "Give us our little one." And they perched on the edge of the cradle and looked tenderly at Keneth. Then he stopped his crying and began to laugh, for these were the voices he knew and loved. And in another minute the gulls had fastened their beaks and claws into the purple cloth, and once more bore him away as they had done when they saved him from the sea.

Out of the door they flew, right over the Shepherd's astonished head, while his wife stared wildly at the empty cradle. And soon Keneth was lying in his own nest on the ledge above the roaring billows.

After this no one tried again to bring the gulls' adopted baby back among human folk. Little Keneth tarried and thrived with his feathered brothers, growing fat and strong. When he came to walk he was somewhat lame, to be sure; one of his legs was shorter than the other, and he limped like a poor gull who has hurt his foot. But this troubled Keneth very little, and the gulls were kind. He was always happy and contented, full of singing and laughter and kind words for all.

And here in his wild, spray-sprinkled nest above the Atlantic breakers, Keneth dwelt all his life. The Welsh peasants of the Gower peninsula revered him as their Saint, knowing him to be a holy man beloved by the gulls and the deer and all the wild creatures of shore and forest, who did their kindly best to make him happy.

Saint Launomar's Cow

Saint Launomar had once been a shepherd boy in the meadows of sunny France, and had lived among the gentle creatures of the fold and byre. So he understood them and their ways very well, and they knew him for their friend. For this is a secret which one cannot keep from the animals whose speech is silent.

Saint Launomar had a cow of whom he was fond, a sleek black and white beauty, who pastured in the green meadows of Chartres near the monastery and came home every evening to be milked and to rub her soft nose against her master's hand, telling him how much she loved him. Mignon was a very wise cow; you could tell that by the curve of her horns and by the wrinkles in her forehead between the eyes; and especially by the way she switched her tail. And indeed, a cow ought to be wise who has been brought up by a whole monastery of learned men, with Launomar, the wisest person in all the country, for her master and friend.

It was a dark night after milking time; Launomar had put Mignon in her stall with a supper of hay before her, and had bade her goodnight and a pleasant cud-time. Then he had shut the heavy barn door and had gone back to his cell to sleep soundly till morning.

But no sooner had his lantern disappeared through the gate of the monastery, than out of the forest came five black figures, creeping, creeping along the wall and across the yard and up to the great oak door. They were all muffled in long black cloaks, and wore their caps pulled down over their faces, as if they were afraid of being recognized. They were wicked-looking men, and they had big knives stuck in their belts quite convenient to their hands. It was a band of robbers; and they had come to steal Launomar's cow, who was known to be the handsomest in all that part of the world.

Very softly they forced open the great door, and very softly they stole across the floor to Mignon's stall and threw a strong halter about her neck to lead her away. But first they were careful to tie up her mouth in a piece of cloth so that she could not low and tell the whole monastery what danger she was in. Mignon was angry, for that was just what she had meant to do as soon as she saw that these were no friends, but wicked men who had come for no good to her or to the monastery.

But now she had to go with them dumbly, although she struggled and kicked and made all the noise she could. But the monks were already sound asleep and snoring on their hard pallets, and never suspected what was going on so near to them. Even Launomar, who turned over in his sleep and murmured, "Ho, Mignon, stand still!" when he dimly recognized a sound of kicking, — even Launomar did not waken to rescue his dear Mignon from the hands of those villains who were taking her away.

The robbers led her hurriedly down the lane, across the familiar meadows and into the dense woods, where they could hide from any one who happened to pass by. Now it was dark and they could see but dimly where they were going. The paths crossed and crisscrossed in so many directions that they soon began to quarrel about which was the right one to take. They did not know this part of the country very well, for they were strangers from a different province, who had come to Launomar's home because they had heard of his famous cow and were bound to have her for themselves.

Very soon the robbers were lost in the tangle of trees and bushes and did not know where they were, or in which direction they ought to go. One said, "Go that way," pointing towards the north. And one said, "No, no! Go that way," pointing directly south. The third grumbled and said, "Ho, fellows! Not so, but this way," and he strode towards the east. While the fourth man cried, "You are all wrong, comrades. It is there we must go," and he started to lead Mignon towards the west. But the fifth robber confessed that indeed he did not know.

"Let us follow the cow," he cried; "she is the only one who can see in the dark. I have always heard that animals will lead you aright if you leave the matter to them." Now as the other robbers really did not have the least idea in the world as to which was the right direction, this seemed to them as sensible a plan as any. So they stripped the halter from Mignon's head and said, "Hi, there! Get along, Cow, and show us the way."

Mignon looked at them through the dark with her big brown eyes, and laughed inside. It seemed too good to be true! They had left her free, and were bidding her to guide them on their way out of the forest back to their own country. Mignon chuckled again, so loudly that they thought she must be choking, and hastily untied the cloth from her mouth. This was just what she wanted, for she longed to chew her cud again. She tossed her head and gave a gentle "Moo!" as if to say, "Come on, simple men, and I will show you the way." But really she was thinking to herself, "Aha! my fine fellows. Now I will lead you a pretty chase. And you shall be repaid for this night's work, aha!"

Mignon was a very wise cow. She had not pastured in the meadows about Chartres with blind eyes. She knew the paths north and south and east and west through the forest and the fern; and even in the dark of the tangled underbrush she could feel out the way quite plainly. But she said to herself, "I must not make the way too easy for these wicked men. I must punish them all I can now that it is my turn."

So she led them roundabout and roundabout, through mud and brambles and swamps; over little brooks and through big miry ponds where they were nearly drowned, — roundabout and roundabout all night long. They wanted to rest, but she went so fast that they could not catch her to make her stand still. And they dared not lose sight of her big whiteness through the dark, for now they were completely lost and could never find their way out of the wilderness without her. So all night long she kept them panting and puffing and wading after her, till they were all worn out, cold and shivering with wet, scratched and bleeding from the briars, and cross as ten sticks.

But when at last, an hour after sunrise, Mignon led them out into an open clearing, their faces brightened.

"Oh, I think I remember this place," said the first man.

"Yes, it has a familiar look. We must be near home," said the second.

"We are at least twenty-five miles from the monks of Chartres by this time," said the third, "and I wish we had some breakfast."

"By another hour we shall have the cow safe in our home den," said the fourth, "and then we will have some bread and milk."

But the fifth interrupted them saying, "Look! Who is that man in gray?" They all looked up quickly and began to tremble; but Mignon gave a great "Moo!" and galloped forward to meet the figure who had stepped out from behind a bush. It was Saint Launomar himself!

He had been up ever since dawn looking for his precious cow; for when he went to milk her he had found the barn empty, and her footprints with those of the five robbers in the moist earth had told the story and pointed which way the company had gone. But it was not his plan to scold or frighten the robbers. He walked up to them, for they were so surprised to see him that they stood still trembling, forgetting even to run away.

"Good-morning, friends," said Launomar kindly. "You have brought back my cow, I see, who to-night for the first time has left her stall to wander far. I thank you, good friends, for bringing Mignon to me. For she is not only a treasure in herself, but she is my dearest friend and I should be most unhappy to lose her."

The men stood staring at Launomar in astonishment. They could hardly believe their eyes and their ears. Where did he come from? What did he mean? But when they realized how kind his voice was, and that he was not accusing them nor threatening to have them punished, they were very much ashamed. They hung their heads guiltily; and then all of a sudden they fell at his feet, the five of them, confessing how it had all come about and begging his pardon.

"We stole the cow, Master," said the first one.

"And carried her these many miles away," said the second.

"We are wicked robbers and deserve to be punished," said the third.

"But we beg you to pardon us," cried the fourth.

"Let us depart, kind Father, we pray you," begged the fifth. "And be so good as to direct us on our way, for we are sorely puzzled."

"Nay, nay," answered Saint Launomar pleasantly, "the cow hath led you a long way, hath she not? You must be both tired and hungry. You cannot journey yet." And in truth they were miserable objects to see, so that the Saint's kind heart was filled with pity, robbers though they were. "Follow me," he said. By this time they were too weak and weary to think of disobeying. So meekly they formed into a procession of seven, Launomar and the cow going cheerfully at the head. For these two were very glad to be together again, and his arm was

Saint Launomar's Cow

thrown lovingly about her glossy neck as they went.

But what was the amazement of the five robbers when in a short minute or two they turned a corner, and there close beside them stood the monastery itself, with the very barn from which they had stolen Mignon the night before! All this time the clever cow had led them in great circles roundabout and roundabout her own home. And after all this scrambling and wading through the darkness, in the morning they were no farther on their journey than they had been at the start. What a wise cow that was! And what a good breakfast of bran porridge and hay and sweet turnips Launomar gave her to pay for her hard night's work.

The five robbers had a good breakfast too; but perhaps they did not relish it as Mignon did hers. For their consciences were heavy; besides, they sat at the monastery table, and all the monks stood by in a row, saying nothing but pursing up their mouths and looking pious; which was trying. And when the robbers came to drink their porridge Launomar said mildly, —

"That is Mignon's milk which you drink, Sirs. It is the best milk in France, and you are welcome to it for your breakfast to-day, since we have such reason to be grateful to you for not putting it beyond our reach forever. Ah, my friends, we could ill spare so worthy a cow, so good a friend, so faithful a guide. But I trust that you will not need her services again. Perhaps by daylight you can find your way home without her if I direct you. The highroad is plain and straight for honest men. I commend it to you."

So, when they were refreshed and rested, Launomar led them forth and pointed out the way as he had promised. He and Mignon stood on the crest of a little hill and watched them out of sight. Then they turned and looked at one another, the wise Saint and his wise cow.

And they both chuckled inside.

Saint Werburgh and Her Goose

Saint Werburgh was a King's daughter, a real princess, and very beautiful. But unlike most princesses of the fairy tales, she cared nothing at all about princes or pretty clothes or jewels, or about having a good time. Her only longing was to do good and to make other people happy, and to grow good and wise herself, so that she could do this all the better. So she studied and studied, worked and worked; and she became a holy woman, an Abbess. And while she was still very young and beautiful, she was given charge of a whole convent of nuns and school-girls not much younger than herself because she was so much wiser and better than any one else in all the countryside.

But though Saint Werburgh had grown so famous and so powerful, she still remained a simple, sweet girl. All the country people loved her, for she was always eager to help them, to cure the little sick children and to advise their fathers and mothers. She never failed to answer the questions which puzzled them, and so she set their poor troubled minds at ease. She was so wise that she knew how to make people do what she knew to be right, even when they wanted to do wrong. And not only human folk but animals felt the power of this young Saint. For she loved and was kind to them also. She studied about them and grew to know their queer habits and their animal way of thinking. And she learned their language, too. Now when one loves a little creature very much and understands it well, one can almost always make it do what one wishes — that is, if one wishes right.

For some time Saint Werburgh had been interested in a flock of wild geese which came every day to get their breakfast in the convent meadow, and to have a morning bath in the pond beneath the window of her cell. She grew to watch until the big, long-necked gray things with their short tails and clumsy feet settled with a harsh "Honk!" in the grass. Then she loved to see the big ones waddle clumsily about in search of dainties for the children, while the babies stood still, flapping their wings and crying greedily till they were fed.

SAINT WERBURGH & HER GOOSE

There was one goose which was her favorite. He was the biggest of them all, fat and happy looking. He was the leader and formed the point of the V in which a flock of wild geese always flies. He was the first to alight in the meadow, and it was he who chose the spot for their breakfast. Saint Werburgh named him Grayking, and she grew very fond of him, although they had never spoken to one another.

Master Hugh was the convent Steward, a big, surly fellow who did not love birds nor animals except when they were served up for him to eat. Hugh also had seen the geese in the meadow. But, instead of thinking how nice and funny they were, and how amusing it was to watch them eat the worms and flop about in the water, he thought only, "What a fine goose pie they would make!" And especially he looked at Grayking, the plumpest and most tempting of them all, and smacked his lips. "Oh, how I wish I had you in my frying-pan!" he said to himself.

Now it happened that worms were rather scarce in the convent meadow that spring. It had been dry, and the worms had crawled away to moister places. So Grayking and his followers found it hard to get breakfast enough. One morning, Saint Werburgh looked in vain for them in the usual spot. At first she was only surprised; but as she waited and waited, and still they did not come, she began to feel much alarmed.

Just as she was going down to her own dinner, the Steward, Hugh, appeared before her cap in hand and bowing low. His fat face was puffed and red with hurrying up the convent hill, and he looked angry.

"What is it, Master Hugh?" asked Saint Werburgh in her gentle voice. "Have you not money enough to buy to-morrow's breakfast?" for it was his duty to pay the convent bills.

"Nay, Lady Abbess," he answered gruffly; "it is not lack of money that troubles me. It is abundance of geese."

"Geese! How? Why?" exclaimed Saint Werburgh, startled. "What of geese, Master Hugh?"

"This of geese, Lady Abbess," he replied. "A flock of long-necked thieves have been in my new-planted field of corn, and have stolen all that was to make my harvest." Saint Werburgh bit her lips.

"What geese were they?" she faltered, though she guessed the truth.

"Whence the rascals come, I know not," he answered, "but this I know. They are the same which gather every morning in the meadow yonder. I spied the leader, a fat, fine thief with a black ring about his neck. It should be a noose, indeed, for hanging. I would have them punished, Lady Abbess."

"They shall be punished, Master Hugh," said Saint Werburgh firmly, and she went sadly up the stair to her cell without tasting so much as a bit of bread for her dinner. For she was sorry to find her friends such naughty birds, and she did not want to punish them, especially Grayking. But she knew that she must do her duty.

When she had put on her cloak and hood she went out into the courtyard behind the convent where there were pens for keeping doves and chickens and little pigs. And standing beside the largest of these pens Saint Werburgh made a strange cry, like the voice of the geese themselves, — a cry which seemed to say, "Come here, Grayking's geese, with Grayking at the head!" And as she stood there waiting, the sky grew black above her head with the shadowing of wings, and the honking of the geese grew louder and nearer till they circled and lighted in a flock at her feet.

She saw that they looked very plump and well-fed, and Grayking was the fattest of the flock. All she did was to look at them steadily and reproachfully; but they came waddling bashfully up to her and stood in a line before her with drooping heads. It seemed as if something made them stay and listen to what she had to say, although they would much rather fly away.

Then she talked to them gently and told them how bad they were to steal corn and spoil the harvest. And as she talked they grew to love her tender voice, even though it scolded them. She cried bitterly as she took each one by the wings and shook him for his sins and whipped him — not too severely. Tears stood in the round eyes of the geese also, not because she hurt them, for she had hardly ruffled their thick feathers; but because they were sorry to have pained the beautiful Saint. For they saw that she loved them, and the more she punished them the better they loved her. Last of all she punished Grayking. But when she had finished she took him up in her arms and kissed him before putting him in the pen with the other geese, where she meant to keep them in prison for a day and a night. Then Grayking hung his head, and in his heart he promised that neither he nor his followers should ever again steal anything, no matter how hungry they were. Now Saint Werburgh read the thought in his heart and was glad, and she smiled as she turned away. She was sorry to keep them in the cage, but she hoped it might do them good. And she said to herself, "They shall have at least one good breakfast of convent porridge before they go."

Saint Werburgh trusted Hugh, the Steward, for she did not yet know the wickedness of his heart. So she told him how she had punished the geese for robbing him, and how she was sure they would never do so any more. Then she bade him see that they had a breakfast of convent porridge the next morning; and after that they should be set free to go where they chose.

Hugh was not satisfied. He thought the geese had not been punished enough. And he went away grumbling, but not daring to say anything cross to the Lady Abbess who was the King's daughter.

II.

Saint Werburgh was busy all the rest of that day and early the next morning too, so she could not get out again to see the prisoned geese. But when she went to her cell for the morning rest after her work was done, she sat down by the window and looked out smilingly, thinking to see her friend Grayking and the others taking their bath in the meadow. But there were no geese to be seen! Werburgh's face grew grave. And even as she sat there wondering what had happened, she heard a prodigious honking overhead, and a flock of geese came straggling down, not in the usual trim V, but all unevenly and without a leader. Grayking was gone!

They fluttered about crying and asking advice of one another, till they heard Saint Werburgh's voice calling them anxiously. Then with a cry of joy they flew straight up to her window and began talking all together, trying to tell her what had happened.

"Grayking is gone!" they said. "Grayking is stolen by the wicked Steward. Grayking was taken away when we were set free, and we shall never see him again. What shall we do, dear lady, without our leader?"

Saint Werburgh was horrified to think that her dear Grayking might be in danger. Oh, how that wicked Steward had deceived her! She began to feel angry. Then she turned to the birds: "Dear geese," she said earnestly, "you have promised me never to steal again, have you not?" and they all honked "Yes!" "Then I will go and question the Steward," she continued, "and if he is guilty I will punish him and make him bring Grayking back to you."

The geese flew away feeling somewhat comforted, and Saint Werburgh sent speedily for Master Hugh. He came, looking much surprised, for he could not imagine what she wanted of him. "Where is the gray goose with the black ring about his neck?" began Saint Werburgh without any preface, looking at him keenly. He stammered and grew confused. "I — I don't know, Lady Abbess," he faltered. He had not guessed that she cared especially about the geese.

"Nay, you know well," said Saint Werburgh, "for I bade you feed them and set them free this morning. But one is gone." "A fox must have stolen it," said he guiltily.

"Ay, a fox with black hair and a red, fat face," quoth Saint Werburgh sternly. "Do not tell me lies. You have taken him, Master Hugh. I can read it in your heart." Then he grew weak and confessed.

"Ay, I have taken the great gray goose," he said faintly. "Was it so very wrong?"

"He was a friend of mine and I love him dearly," said Saint Werburgh. At these words the Steward turned very pale indeed.

"I did not know," he gasped.

"Go and bring him to me, then," commanded the Saint, and pointed to the door. Master Hugh slunk out looking very sick and miserable and horribly frightened. For the truth was that he had been tempted by Grayking's fatness. He had carried the goose home and made him into a hot, juicy pie which he had eaten for that very morning's breakfast. So how could he bring the bird back to Saint Werburgh, no matter how sternly she commanded?

All day long he hid in the woods, not daring to let himself be seen by any one. For Saint Werburgh was a King's daughter; and if the King should learn what he had done to the pet of the Lady Abbess, he might have Hugh himself punished by being baked into a pie for the King's hounds to eat.

But at night he could bear it no longer. He heard the voice of Saint Werburgh calling his name very softly from the convent, "Master Hugh, Master Hugh, come, bring me my goose!" And just as the geese

Saint Werburgh and Her Goose

could not help coming when she called them, so he felt that he must go, whether he would or no. He went into his pantry and took down the remains of the great pie. He gathered up the bones of poor Grayking in a little basket, and with chattering teeth and shaking limbs stole up to the convent and knocked at the wicket gate.

Saint Werburgh was waiting for him. "I knew you would come," she said. "Have you brought my goose?" Then silently and with trembling hands he took out the bones one by one and laid them on the ground before Saint Werburgh. So he stood with bowed head and knocking knees waiting to hear her pronounce his punishment

"Oh, you wicked man!" she said sadly. "You have killed my beautiful Grayking, who never did harm to any one except to steal a little corn."

"I did not know you loved him, Lady," faltered the man in self-defense.

"You ought to have known it," she returned; "you ought to have loved him yourself."

"I did, Lady Abbess," confessed the man. "That was the trouble. I loved him too well — in a pie."

"Oh, selfish, gluttonous man!" she exclaimed in disgust. "Can you not see the beauty of a dear little live creature till it is dead and fit only for your table? I shall have you taught better. Henceforth you shall be made to study the lives and ways of all things which live about the convent; and never again, for punishment, shall you eat flesh of any bird or beast. We will see if you cannot be taught to love them when they have ceased to mean Pie. Moreover, you shall be confined for two days and two nights in the pen where I kept the geese. And porridge shall be your only food the while. Go, Master Hugh."

So the wicked Steward was punished. But he learned his lesson; and after a little while he grew to love the birds almost as well as Saint Werburgh herself.

But she had not yet finished with Grayking. After Master Hugh had gone she bent over the pitiful little pile of bones which was all that was left of that unlucky pie. A tear fell upon them from her beautiful eyes; and kneeling down she touched them with her white fingers, speaking softly the name of the bird whom she had loved.

"Grayking, arise," she said. And hardly had the words left her mouth when a strange thing happened. The bones stirred, lifted themselves, and in a moment a glad "Honk!" sounded in the air, and Grayking himself, black ring and all, stood ruffling his feathers before her. She clasped him in her arms and kissed him again and again. Then calling the rest of the flock by her strange power, she showed them their lost leader restored as good as new.

What a happy flock of geese flew honking away in an even V, with the handsomest, grayest, plumpest goose in all the world at their head! And what an exciting story he had to tell his mates! Surely, no other goose ever lived who could tell how it felt to be made into pie, to be eaten and to have his bones picked clean by a greedy Steward.

This is how Saint Werburgh made lifelong friendship with a flock of big gray geese. And I dare say even now in England one of their descendants may be found with a black ring around his neck, the handsomest, grayest, plumpest goose in all the world. And when he hears the name of Saint Werburgh, which has been handed down to him from grandfather to grandson for twelve hundred years, he will give an especially loud "Honk!" of praise.

Dear Saint Werburgh! One would almost be willing to make a goose of himself if so he might see her again, with all her feathered friends about her.

The Ballad of Saint Athracta's Stags

Athracta was a maiden fair,
    A Prince's daughter she;
Down to her feet fell golden hair,
    A wondrous sight to see.

And all amid this golden shower,
    The sweetest rosebud face
Blossomed like a dew-fed flower
    Upon a stem of grace.

Yet loved she not the court of kings,
    But in the wild would be,
With but one maid her hair to braid
    And bear her company.

So, near Lough Cara's silver sheen,
    They built of turf and bark
A hut wherein from springtide green
    They dwelt through winter's dark.

On seven cross-roads the hut was made,
    That they might offer rest
To pilgrims by the night waylaid,
    And strangers hunger-pressed.

To draw them water from the lake,
    To till their little soil,
Two ancient horses did they take,
    Outworn for other toil.

Once gallant chargers these had been,
    Keen-eyed and prancing gay,
Who tourneys brave and wars had seen,

All decked in bright array.

But now their age in peace was spent
    By kind Athracta's side;
No gallant wars, no tournament,
    And yet they served with pride.

Their neighbors in the forest glades
    Were stately, antlered deer,
Nor of the two most holy maids
    Had these, their brothers, fear.

So dwelt the maidens there alone
    For many months and years,
The doings of the world unknown,
    Its wars, its woes, its tears.

But strife was stirring in the land,
    And kings must castles build,
To guard them from the foeman's hand
    With fire and weapon filled.

And so the King's most stern decree
    Went forth upon a day, —
"My serfs must build a fort for me,
    Each must his service pay.

"Each man and maiden must fulfill
    In this great work his share;
It is the King of Connaught's will,
    Let tardy hands beware!"

Athracta sent unto the King:
    "We be but maidens twain,
My Liege, we cannot do this thing,
    I beg we may refrain."

The Ballad of Saint Athracta's Stags

But sternly sent he back the word, —
    "Ye maids must do your part."
He was a hard and cruel lord,
    No pity touched his heart.

So forth they fared into the wood,
    Athracta with her maid,
To fell the timber as they could,
    Without of men for aid.

Heavy the axe and full of pain
    Each weak and skill-less stroke,
Yet strove the maids again, again,
    With walnut, beech, and oak.

Until upon the wagon cast
    By which the horses stood,
Their bleeding hands had piled at last
    The goodly logs of wood.

But when Athracta saw the steeds
    Straining with feeble will
To draw the heavy load, it needs
    Must make her eyes to fill.

Athracta spoke all piteously, —
    "Alack ! poor broken things,
Must you, too, bear your painful share
    To save the pride of Kings?

"How can I ease your burden, how,
    My faithful servants still?
My little hands are bleeding now
    With toil beyond their skill."

"O mistress dear," then spoke her maid,
    "These be but feeble nags;

How would the King's pride be dismayed
    If you could harness Stags!"

"Thou sayest well," Athracta vowed.
    "Come hither, Stags!" she cried,
And lo! the thud of hoofs grew loud
    Ere yet the echo died.

"Come hither, Stags!" O'er green and glade
    The silver summons thrilled,
And soon the space about the maid
    With antlered kings was filled.

Through moss and fern and tangled trees
    Twelve panting creatures broke,
And bending low their stately knees
    They knelt beneath the yoke.

Now harnessed in the horses' stead
    The great Stags strained their best,
To please the Lady at their head
    And follow her behest.

But lo! a vexing thing then happed;
    Scarce had they gained the road,
The rusty chains of iron snapped
    Beneath the heavy load.

Yet paused she not in weak despair,
    This noble-hearted maid,
But loosed her heavy golden hair
    Out from its double braid.

She loosed her locks so wonder-bright
    And shook them to the breeze; —
It seemed a beam of yellow light
    Had sifted through the trees.

The Ballad of Saint Athracta's Stags

Then from amid this golden net
    She plucked some silken strands,
And where the chains had first been set
    She bound them with her hands.

She tied the ends against the strain,
    And knotted them with care,
Then bade the Stags pull once again
    Upon the ropes of hair.

And lo! the slender harness held,
    And lo! the antlered steeds
Went forth to prove their generous love
    Lent to a maiden's needs.

Straight to the King her gift they bore
    To fill his heart with shame;
And her true maiden went before
    To show him whence they came.

Now when the King this wonder saw
    He turned all pale and red,
"She hath a greater power than law,"
    He vowed, and bowed his head.

"She hath a greater power than I,
    Whose slaves the wild stags be,
And golden hair like this might snare
    E'en the wild heart of me.

"No need to her of castles stout,
    No need of moat or tower,
With antlered guardians about
    Her lonely wild-wood bower.

"No need to her of watch or ward,
    With friends like these at hand;

Bid her from me henceforth to be
   Queen of her little land.

"Henceforth she is no serf of mine,
   Nor subject to my throne;
Where'er her golden hair may shine
   That is her realm alone."

So where the seven cross-roads met
   Still dwelt the holy maid,
Her hut a place of refuge set
   For all who shelter prayed.

Her realm a holy place of peace,
   Where, with the ancient nags,
Lived out their days in pleasant ways
   Athracta's faithful Stags.

Saint Kentigern and the Robin

Once upon a time Saint Servan kept a school near Glasgow in Scotland, and many boys, big and little, came there to study. Now of all these boys there was one who surpassed the rest in everything that makes a good scholar. Kentigern was one of the smallest boys in the school, and yet he stood at the head of all his classes. It was Kentigern who found the answer to the knottiest problem, and who read off the hardest passages of Latin when no one else was able to make sense of them. It was Kentigern who learned his lessons first and who recited them best. It was Kentigern who sang the loudest and was never off the pitch; and good Saint Servan loved him best of all his pupils.

For all these reasons, and for several more like them, the other boys were jealous of Kentigern and did everything they could to trouble him and make him unhappy. They tried to make him fail in his lessons by talking and laughing when it was his turn to recite. But this was a useless trick; his answers were always ready, so they had to give this up. They teased him and called him names, trying to make him lose his temper so that he would be punished. But he was too good-natured to be cross with them; so they had to give this up. They tried to coax him into mischief and lead him do something which would make Saint Servan angry with him. But Kentigern loved his master too well to do anything to trouble him. So the boys had finally to give this up also.

There was only one way to bring Kentigern into disgrace. They must plan a trap, and make him fall into it. For weeks they racked their brains trying to think what they should do; but at last they thought they had hit upon a plan.

It was all concerned with a fire. In those days there were no matches with which to strike a light in a second. Matches had not been invented in the year 600, nor indeed for many centuries afterwards. Their way of making a fire was by rubbing two dry sticks together until they grew hot and a spark fell out upon the wood which was to be kindled.

And this was a very difficult and tiresome thing to do, especially in the winter when there were few dry sticks to be found. So the fire which was kept burning night and day in the great fireplace of Saint Servan's school was tended carefully, and it would be a very serious thing to let this go out. For how would the breakfast be cooked, and the rooms warmed, and the candles lighted for the morning service in the chapel if there were no fire on the great hearth?

So for a week at a time the boys had to take turns in tending the fire; and the boy whose turn it was had to rise at midnight and put on wood enough to keep the blaze bright until morning. And oh! how angry Saint Servan would be with any boy who was so careless as to let the fire go out in the night.

Now it was Kentigern's week to tend the fire; and for several days he did tend it faithfully. But the boys were waiting for a chance to play their mean trick. On the fourth night Kentigern rose as the chapel clock boomed "twelve!" and went down to the kitchen to give the hungry fire its midnight lunch of snappy wood. But as soon as he stepped into the great empty hall he knew that something was wrong. Br-r-r! The air was damp and chilly, and there was no crimson glow on the hearthstones. Kentigern shivered and ran to the fireplace, peering into the black cavern. There was nothing but a heap of white ashes and half-burnt wood!

Then Kentigern's heart sank, for he knew he should be blamed for carelessness, although he suspected that some one had thrown water on the fire and put it out. And he guessed that it was the other boys who had done this spiteful thing to bring him into trouble. He did not know what to do. But a sudden courage came to him. He took up a log of wood from the corner and laid it on the heap of ashes. Then bending down he blew gently on the pile. And oh, wonderful to say! It was as if he had scratched a dozen cards of matches and had touched them to a pile of paper. Hardly had his breath stirred the ashes and made the moss shiver on the great log, when the whole fireplace was filled with dancing flames, and the wood began to snap and crack in the best kind of a blaze. Kentigern laughed softly to himself as he stole back to bed, and said never a word to the sleeping boys who had tried to make mischief for him.

When they woke in the morning they began to chuckle and nudge

Saint Kentigern and the Robin

one another, expecting every moment to see Saint Servan come frowning in search of the careless Kentigern. And every boy was ready to declare that the fire was burning brightly when he went to bed, and that Kentigern had forgotten to go down and tend it at midnight. But they were prevented from telling this falsehood. For the bell rang as usual for breakfast, and down they all went to find a beautiful fire burning on the hearth, and Kentigern going with his taper to light the chapel candelabra. They did not know how it had happened till long, long afterwards when Kentigern had made many other wonders come to pass, and when he was known far and wide as a Saint even wiser than Servan his master.

But meanwhile the boys hated him more than ever, when they saw how much better Saint Servan loved him every day. And once more they planned to bring him into disgrace. But this time it was an even more cruel thing which they meant to do. For if they succeeded it would not only cause Kentigern to be punished and make Saint Servan unhappy, but it would cost the life of an innocent little creature who never had done any .harm to a single one of them.

Saint Servan was a kind-hearted old man, and he had a Robin Redbreast of which he was very fond, — a black-eyed fellow who ate his breakfast out of the Saint's hand. And when the master chanted the Psalms the little chorister would perch on Servan's shoulder and flap his wings, twittering as if he were trying to join in the songs of praise.

Now one morning when the coast was clear, the boys killed the little Redbreast and pulled off his head. And then the biggest boy of them all took the dead bird in his hand, and followed by all the rest ran screaming to Saint Servan himself pretending to feel very sorry.

"Oh Father!" cried the Big Boy, "just see what the wicked Kentigern has done! Look at your Robin whom Kentigern has killed!"

Then they all began to cry out against Kentigern, and some even declared that they had seen him do the wicked deed; which was a horrid story, and their tongues must have smarted well as they spoke it.

Of course Saint Servan was very sad and angry. He tenderly took the little limp body in his hand and went to seek Kentigern, the other boys tiptoeing after him to see the fun. And by and by they came

47

SAINT KENTIGERN & THE ROBIN

upon him in a window bending over a big book which he was studying. Saint Servan strode up to him and laid a heavy hand upon his shoulder.

"Look at this, boy," he cried with a sad voice, "look at this cruel

Saint Kentigern and the Robin

deed, and tell me what shall be done to punish the slayer? Did I not love the Robin, even as I loved you, ungrateful boy!"

Kentigern turned quite pale with surprise and sorrow, and the tears came into his eyes.

"Oh, the dear little bird," he said. "Did I not love him too? Who has killed him, Father?"

"You did, you did; we saw you!" cried all the boys in a chorus.

Kentigern turned and looked at them in astonishment. He did not say a word, but his cheeks grew red and his eyes flashed. This was more than even his patience could stand.

"Well, what have you to say for yourself?" queried Saint Servan sternly. Kentigern turned to him sadly.

"Oh Father!" he said, "how can you believe that I would do such a cruel thing, to hurt the bird and to make you sad? I did not do it, Father."

"Can you prove it?" asked Saint Servan still more sternly, for he thought the boy was telling a falsehood to hide his guilt.

"Give me the Robin, Father," said Kentigern, holding out his hand. "I will prove that it was not this hand which cowardly used so small a thing as a tiny bird." Then holding the limp body in one hand and the downy head in the other, he stood before them all, looking up towards heaven, and made his little prayer.

"O Father in heaven," he said, "prove to my dear Father on earth that I have not done this cruel thing. If I am innocent, give me power to undo the wrong and restore life to the little singer who loved to praise Thee with his sweet voice." Then gently he set the head in place where it should be and, as his tears fell upon the Robin's neck, it seemed to grow again to the body. The feathers ruffled and the limp wings fluttered feebly; the black eyes opened, and out of the bill came a little chirp. Then the Robin hopped out of Kentigern's hands and across the floor to Saint Servan's feet, and flew up on his master's shoulder. There he sat and sang such a carol of joy as made the great hall ring again. But all the guilty boys put their fingers in their ears and turned pale, as if they understood what he was saying, and as if it told the truth about their jealousy and their cruelty and their falsehood.

So Saint Servan learned that Kentigern was innocent, and saw how it had all happened. The real culprits were severely punished. But Kentigern became even dearer than before to his master, who helped him in every way to become the great and famous Saint he afterwards was. And the Robin was another fond and faithful friend. For the bird seemed never to forget that Kentigern had restored his life, and always sang his sweetest song for the boy.

You may be sure that after this the boys gave up trying to get the better of Kentigern. They had learned that lesson, and thenceforth they were more kind and respectful to a boy over whom some kind Power seemed to keep special charge.

Saint Blaise and His Beasts

This is the story of a Saint who loved all animals and whom the animals therefore loved in return. Saint Blaise was the son of wealthy people in Sebaste, a town of Armenia near Turkey, in the days when it was fashionable to be a heathen. He was not like the other boys, his playmates, for he was a Christian, full of sympathy for everything that lived. More than all things he longed to learn how to help the creatures that he loved, — men and women, the children, the dumb beasts, and everything that suffered and was sick. So he went to school and studied medicine; and by and by he grew up to be a wise man with a big, tender heart. Every one loved him, for he did great good among the people of his village, tending their children and healing their cattle and household pets.

Nor did he neglect even the wild beasts. For Saint Blaise loved to go away into the woods and fields where he could learn about the untamed creatures and teach them to be his friends. The birds and beasts and fishes grew to love him because he never hurt them, but talked to them kindly and healed them when they were sick or wounded. The timid creatures were brave in his presence, and the fierce ones grew tame and gentle at the sound of his voice. The little birds brought him food, and the four-footed beasts ran errands and were his messengers. The legends say that they used to visit him in his forest home, which was a cave on Mount Argus near the city of Sebaste. Every morning they came to see how their master was faring, to receive his blessing and lick his hands in gratitude. If they found the Saint at his prayers they never disturbed him, but waited in a patient, wistful group at the door of his cave until he rose from his knees.

One day a poor woman came to him in great distress because a wolf had carried away her pig. Saint Blaise was sorry to hear that one of his friends had done so wicked a thing. He bade the woman go home, and said he would see what could be done. He called the Wolf up to him and shook his head gravely at the culprit.

"You bad Wolf!" he said. "Don't you know that the Pig was a friend of mine, too? He is not handsome, but he is nice and plump; and he is the only pig of a poor, lone woman. How could you be so selfish? Go straight home and get my friend Pig, and drive him down to the woman's house." Then the Wolf went sheepishly away, and did what the good Saint had told him to do; for the Pig had not yet been made into pork. And when the poor woman saw the Pig run grunting into her yard, chased by the repentant Wolf, she fell upon his fat neck and wept tears of joy. Then the Wolf went back to Saint Blaise, who told him he was a good wolf, and gave him a dish of fresh milk to cool his throat.

Saint Blaise was chosen Bishop by the Christians who loved him for his piety and his charity. And the wood-beasts were glad of this honor done to their dear master. But the poor creatures did not know how dangerous it was to be a Christian in those days, and especially to be a Bishop who had much power over the people. For the heathen were jealous of him, and feared that he would make all the people Christians too, when they saw the wonderful cures which his medicines made. But they could not find him, for he was living in his forest cave.

This was 316 years after Christ's birth, and the cruel Emperor Licinius was causing many Christians to be killed. Agricola was the governor whom Licinius had appointed in Sebaste, and he sent his soldiers into the mountains to get some wild beasts for the games in the arena, where the Christians were to be put to death. But they could not find any beasts at all in the mountains, or in the fields, or valleys, or woods. They thought this very strange. But by and by they came by accident to the cave where Saint Blaise lived.

And there were the animals, all the fierce beasts whom they feared; lions, tigers, leopards, bears, and wolves, making their morning call upon Saint Blaise and sitting quietly about. In the midst was Blaise himself praying so earnestly that he never noticed the men with nets and spears who had come to entrap the beasts. Although the creatures were frightened they did not move nor growl for fear of disturbing their master, but kept quite still, glaring at the soldiers with big yellow eyes. The men were so astonished at the sight that they stole away without capturing an animal or saying a word to Saint Blaise, for they thought he must be Orpheus or some heathen

Saint Blaise and His Beasts

god who charmed wild beasts. They went to the Governor and told him what they had seen, and he said, —

"Ho! I know he is a Christian. The Christians and the beasts are great friends. Go and bring him to me straightway."

And this time the soldiers went in the afternoon when the animals were taking their after-dinner nap. So they found Saint Blaise quite alone, again at his devotions. They told him he must come with them; but instead of being frightened he said joyfully, "I am ready, I have long expected you." For he was a holy man willing to die for his faith, and holy men often knew what was going to happen to them.

It was on his way to prison that Saint Blaise cured his last patient, — a sick child whose mother brought him to the holy man's feet begging help. The child had swallowed a bone and was choking to death, poor little thing. But Saint Blaise touched the baby's throat and the trouble was gone. This is why in olden times people with sore throats always prayed to Saint Blaise to make them well.

The good Bishop was put in prison. And after that they tortured him, trying to make him promise not to be a Christian any longer. But Saint Blaise refused to become a heathen and to sacrifice to the gods. And so they determined that he must die. They would have put him in the arena with the wild beasts, but they knew that these faithful creatures would not harm their friend. The beasts could not save him from the cruel men, but at least they would not do anything to hurt him. Those which were still left in the forest howled and moaned about his deserted cave, and went sniffing and searching for him everywhere, like stray dogs who have lost their master. It was a sad day for the wood-creatures when Saint Blaise was taken from them forever.

The soldiers were told to drown Saint Blaise in the neighboring lake. But he made the sign of the Cross as they cast him from the boat, and the water bore him up, so that he walked upon it as if it were a floor, just as Christ did once upon the Sea of Galilee. When the soldiers tried to do the same, however, thinking to follow and recapture him, they sank and were drowned. At last of his own free will Saint Blaise walked back to the shore, clothed in light and very beautiful to look upon; for he was ready and eager to die. He let the heathen seize him, and soon after this was beheaded.

In very old times it used to be the custom in England on the third of February to light great bonfires on all the hills, — blazes in honor of his name.

And we can well believe that all the little animals came out of their dens and burrows and nests at the sight of these fires, and thought with loving hearts of the dear old Saint who so many years ago used to be kind to their ancestors, the beasts in the forests of Armenia.

Saint Cuthbert's Peace

Saint Cuthbert was a Scotch shepherd boy who tended his flocks along the river Tweed near Melrose. Night and day he lived in the open air, drinking in the sunshine and sleeping on the heather. And he grew up big and strong and handsome, — the finest lad in all that part of the country. He could run faster than any one, and was always the champion in the wrestling matches to which he challenged the village boys for miles around. And you should have seen him turn somersaults and walk on his hands! No one in all the world could beat him at that. Saint Cuthbert lived more than a thousand years ago, and yet the people of Scotland still tell tales of his strength and agility and grace in games with the other boys. He was their leader and chief, and every one was sure that he would grow up to be a famous man.

But he tended his sheep faithfully until the time came. For he was growing and learning all the while. In his happy outdoor life he became wise in many things which other people never know. He found the secret of the whispering wind, and the song of the brook. He knew what the chatter of the squirrels meant, and the caw of the crows. He learned the ways of all the little bright-eyed animals whom he met in his walks over the hills of heather; and he grew to love every creature which has fur or feathers and goes upon four legs or on two. Especially he loved the birds. He used to watch them for hours together, the little larks gurgling up and trilling down again; the great gulls swooping and curling and sailing like white ships in the blue sea of sky. And he longed, oh! how he longed to have wings and to flutter and float away like the birds.

One night while he lay watching his sheep upon the pink heather which bears you up like a springy cushion, he saw a strange thing in the sky. There seemed a great pathway of light, and down it a band of angels came from heaven, clothed all in rainbow glory. And in a little while he saw them mounting back again, bearing a beautiful blossom among them. And he guessed that it was the soul of some holy man, being carried to Paradise.

Saints and Friendly Beasts

SAINT CUTHBERT'S VISION

Sure enough, the next day the news went abroad that Aidan, the holy Bishop of Lindisfarne, had died that very night. Then Cuthbert knew that he, a little shepherd boy, had been blessed to see a holy vision. He wondered why; but he felt sure that it meant some special grace to him. Day after day, night after night, he thought about it, wondering and wondering. And at last he made up his mind that he, too, would become a holy man, and then perhaps he should find out all about it.

He was fifteen years old when he came to Melrose Abbey to be made a monk. And there he lived and grew rich with the wisdom of books; which, added to the wisdom of the woods and hills and streams which he already possessed, made him a very wise man indeed.

He had not been there long before every one, even the Abbot himself, saw that this glorious young monk was the most powerful of them all. Every one obeyed and reverenced him. Every one came to ask his advice and help. Every one sent for him in time of trouble. With his beautiful face and strong body, his kind eyes and great hands tender as a woman's to touch a little sick child, he was loved by the people in all the country around. For he had the great gift of sympathy. In those years while he had lived under the kind, hot sun his heart had grown mellow and soft like a ripe apple.

Many of the people in the far-off hills and lonely Scotch moorlands were like savages, wild and timid, hating every stranger. But the hearts of these poor children of the heather warmed to the big brother who came among them with love shining in his eyes and a desire to help them. He used to trudge into the wildest, most distant places to reach them, to teach and comfort them. He was always carrying food and clothing to the poor and medicine to the sick, for he could not bear to see others suffer. But he was not afraid of suffering himself.

One thing Cuthbert used to do which showed how strong and healthy he was. Even until he grew to be quite an old man he used to take a bath in the sea every day of his life. No matter how cold it was he would plunge into the waves and come out all dripping upon the frozen beach, where he would always kneel and say a little prayer before going home.

One bitter night in winter as Cuthbert knelt thus in the snow after his plunge, blue with cold, two brown otters came up out of the sea and stole to Cuthbert's side. And as he prayed, not noticing them at all, they licked his poor frozen feet, trying to warm them, and rubbed against him with their thick, soft fur till he was dry again. Thus the water-creatures did their little best for him who loved them and who had done so much for others.

When the Abbot Boswell died Cuthbert became head of the Abbey in his place. But after twelve years of living indoors with the other monks he could bear it no longer. For he longed to get out into the fresh air and under the sky once more. He resolved to become a hermit, and to live a wild outdoor life with the birds whom he loved.

He built his nest on a wild little island named Farne, a steep, rocky sea-mountain where ten or fifteen years before had lived that same holy Aidan whose passage to heaven he had witnessed when he was a shepherd boy at Melrose. The nest was really a hole in the ground — you know some birds build so. He dug himself a round cell in the rock, the roof having a window open to his dear sky. The walls were of turf and stone and it was thatched with straw. There were two rooms, one where he lived and slept and cooked; the other for his little chapel, where he sang praises like any bird and sat for hours thinking holy thoughts. Before the door he hung an ox-hide, and this was his only protection from the winds of the sea. He found a spring in the rock and this supplied him with water; and he planted a plot of barley which yielded him food.

Thus he lived, alone with the birds which swarmed about the rock. The winds swept over him and the waves curled and broke almost at the door of his hut, but he did not care. Indeed, the sea was a rough friend to him. Once when by mistake it came too near and washed away part of the cottage, Cuthbert sent to his brother monks on the mainland, asking them to bring him a beam to prop up the roof, for there was no wood on his rocky isle. But this the brothers forgot to do. The sea, however, seemed sorry for having been so careless, and at the next high tide it washed up at the Saint's feet the beam he wished.

He did not lack for friends. For, as soon as he made this island rock his home, it became the haunt of every kind of bird. The other animals could not reach him from the shore, poor things. But the blessed wings of the gulls and curlews, the eider-ducks and the ravens, bore them to their Master in his retreat.

"Hi!" they said to one another, "we have got him to ourselves now.

Those poor, featherless creatures can't come here, neither can he get away, without wings. He is all our own now!"

This was not quite true, for they forgot that though men cannot fly they make boats with wings, and so can cross the sea. Cuthbert often went ashore to do errands of mercy, in peasants' huts and in the Queen's palace. And many people came to see him also, because his fame had spread over the kingdom. He made them welcome to the house which he had built for his guests as far as possible from his own solitary cell. He loved them, and helped them when he could. But after all, the birds were his dearest friends, and he liked best to be alone with them.

They would come and sit upon his shoulders and knees and let him take them up and caress them. They followed him in flocks when he went to walk. They watched at the door of his hut and ate breakfast, dinner, and supper with him. Many people believed that every day the birds brought him food from Paradise, but this story arose, as so many false stories do, from another thing that really happened. For once when some blackbirds thoughtlessly stole his barley and some of the straw from his roof, Cuthbert scolded them, and bade them never to do so again. It made the birds ashamed, and to show that they were sorry they brought him a great lump of suet. He did not eat it, however, as they expected he would, but used it to grease his shoes with, and it lasted a long time.

Now Cuthbert loved all these birds dearly, especially the unselfish eider-duck who picks the down from her own breast to make a softer bed for her little ones. He was kind to them and they had no fear of him. But he dreaded lest after he was gone others should be less kind to his pets. So to protect them he made a promise, and he bequeathed them a legacy, the gift of Saint Cuthbert's Peace. He promised that no one should harm or kill them on that island without being dreadfully punished. And he gave them this Peace for ever and ever. So that thenceforth ill befell whoever injured one of Saint Cuthbert's birds. There are two stories to prove this, and they both happened long after Cuthbert was gone from Fame.

Now Liveing was the servant of Ælric, the hermit who next dwelt in Cuthbert's cell. And one day while Ælric was gone away to the mainland, Liveing killed and ate one of the eider-ducks who still lived

Saints and Friendly Beasts

and built their nests near the hut where the Saint had lived. Liveing knew the promise of Saint Cuthbert's Peace, but he thought that no one would find out his crime. For he scattered the bones and feathers over the cliff, and saw them washed away by the waves. But after Ælric, his master, came back, he found a lump of bones and feathers rolled together and cast by the tide upon the very steps of his chapel. For even the sea was promised to Saint Cuthbert's Peace, and had to betray the guilty man. So Liveing was discovered and punished.

And this is the second story. The birds themselves were bound by the Peace to be kind to one another. The big birds were forbidden to hurt or kill a little one. And this is what happened to a great hawk who flapped over from the neighboring island of Lindisfarne and ate up the tame sparrow which belonged to Bartholomew, another hermit who lived after Ælric at Farne. For Saint Cuthbert's power made the hawk fly for days around and around the island, never able to get away, never able to stop, though he was ready to drop with weariness and hunger. He would have kept on flying until now, or until he fell into the sea and was drowned, if at last the hermit had not taken pity upon him. Bartholomew caught the tired hawk by his wings and carried him to the seashore, and there in Saint Cuthbert's name he bade him fly away, and never come back to Farne to bother him and his peaceful birds.

So Saint Cuthbert lived on his island surrounded by his feathered friends. He never grew proud, though every one loved and reverenced him and called him a Saint. He was always poor, although royal ladies, even the Queen herself made him presents of gold and jewels, — which he gave away to the needy. He was always meek, though Egfried the King himself came all the way to Farne to make him a grand Bishop, kneeling on the ground before Cuthbert and begging him to accept the gift. His life was like a beacon to men, burning bright and clear. And after he died a lighthouse was built on his rock to be a spark of hope for the sailors at sea.

As for Saint Cuthbert's Peace, it still blesses the lonely rock of Farne. Flocks of sea-birds swarm about it, descendants of those who knew the Saint himself. They are tame and gentle and suspect no harm from any one, for have they not the promise of their Saint? Alas! Men less kindly than he have forgotten the promise and have broken the Peace. They have killed many of the trusting birds who let them come up close and take them in their hands, expecting to be petted. For the birds never even thought to run away, poor, innocent, soft-eyed creatures. And how cruelly they were deceived!

But I am sure that Saint Cuthbert's dreadful charm still binds the murderers. He will not forget his promise; and though they may not be punished immediately, as Liveing was, nor suffer like the wicked hawk, Saint Cuthbert will bring sorrow upon their heads at last and misfortune to the cruel hands which dare to hurt his birds.

The Ballad of Saint Felix

It was in sunny Italy
    Where skies are blue and fair,
Where little birds sing all the day,
    And flowers scent the air.

But sorrow was through all the land,
    And bloody deeds, and strife,
For the cruel heathen Emperor
    Was slaying Christian life.

And Nola of Campania
    Was full of soldiers grim,
Who sought where good Saint Felix dwelt,
    To be the death of him.

For he, the Bishop, old and wise,
    Was famous far and near,
And to the troubled Christian folk
    His name was passing dear.

Saint Felix would not run away,
    But thought no shame to hide
Until the bloody storm passed o'er,
    And he might safely bide.

And so he doffed his Bishop's robe,
    And donned a Pilgrim's dress,
With hat and staff and sandal-shoon,
    So none his name would guess.

Now as Saint Felix, bent and gray,
    Was tottering down the street,
A band of soldiers, fierce and wild,
    The old man chanced to meet

"Ho! Pilgrim," cried the Captain stern,
    Who stopped him with his sword,
"Answer me truly, or thy life
    Shall pay the lying word.

"We sought for Felix at his home,
    We find him not, alas!
Say, hast thou met him, for within
    The hour he did pass?

"Say, hast thou met him? Tell us true,
    Or thou shalt lose thy head."
Saint Felix looked him in the eyes,
    "I met him not," he said.

So then the soldiers let him pass, —
    But he had spoken truth, —
And hurried forward on their search,
    A fruitless quest, in sooth!

And good Saint Felix hastened too,
    As quickly as he might,
For they would guess full soon, he knew,
    How he had tricked their sight

And truly, ere his oaken staff
    Had helped his feeble feet
To win a mile, he heard their shouts
    A-nearing down the street.

The Ballad of Saint Felix

He heard the clashing of their swords,
    Their voices' cruel roar,
Alack! the chase was almost done,
    For he could speed no more.

All breathless, worn, and clean forspent
    He looked about him there;
He spied a tiny ray of hope,
    And made a little prayer.

There was a broken, ruined wall
    That crumbled by the road,
And through a cleft Saint Felix crept,
    And in a corner bode.

It was a sorry hiding-place,
    That scarce could hope to 'scape
The keen sight of those bloody men,
    For murder all agape.

But lo! in answer to his prayer
    Made in the Holy Name,
To help Saint Felix in his need
    A little spider came.

And there across the narrow hole
    Through which Saint Felix fled,
The spider spun a heavy web
    Out of her silken thread.

So fast she spun, so faithfully,
    That when the soldiers came
To pause beside the ruined wall
    And shout the Bishop's name,

They found a silken curtain there
   Wherethrough they could not see;
And "Ho!" they said, "he is not here,
   Look, look! it cannot be;

"No one has passed this spider's web
   For many and many a day,
See, men, how it is thick and strong;"
   And so they went away.

And this is how Saint Felix fared
   To 'scape the threatened doom,
Saved by a little spider's web,
   Spun from her wondrous loom.

For when the soldiers all had passed
   It luckily befell,
Among the ruins of the walls
   He found a half-dug well.

And there he hid for many months,
   Safe from the eager eyes
Of all those cruel soldier-men
   And money-seeking spies.

And on the eve when this thing happed,
   It chanced a Christian dame
Was passing by the ruined wall
   Calling her Bishop's name.

For well she knew he must be hid,
   And came to bring him food;
And so he answered from the well,
   Saint Felix, old and good.

The Ballad of Saint Felix

And for the many weary months
    She came there, day by day,
All stealthily to bring him bread,
    So no one guessed the way.

And when at last the peace was made,
    Saint Felix left his well.
What welcome of his folk he had
    There are no words to tell!

Saint Fronto's Camels

This is a story of Egypt. In the midst of a great yellow sea of sand was a tiny green island of an oasis. Everywhere else the sunlight burned on sand and rocks and low, bare hills to the west. But here there was shade under the palm-trees, and a spring of cool, clear water. It seemed a pleasant place, but the men who were living here were far from happy. There was grumbling and discontent; there were sulky looks and frowns. Yet these men were trying to be holy hermits, to live beautiful lives and forget how to be selfish. But it is hard to be good when one is starving.

There were seventy of them in this lonely camp in the desert, — seventy hungry monks, who for many days had had only a few olives to eat. And they blamed one man for all their suffering. It was Fronto who had induced them to leave the pleasant monastery at Nitria, where the rest of their brethren were living in peace and plenty. It was Fronto who had led them into this miserable desert to serve God in solitude, as holy men loved to do in the early days of Christendom.

Fronto was a holy man, full of faith and courage. He had promised that they should be fed and cared for in the desert even though they took no care for themselves, and they had believed him. So each monk took a few olives in his pouch and a double-pronged hoe to dig and plant corn with, and followed Fronto into the desert.

After trudging many days they found this spot, far to the east, where no caravans would come to interrupt them, for it was out of the way of travel. But soon also they found their provisions gone and no others forthcoming. What were they to do? They asked Fronto, but he only bade them be patient. It was when they had borne the pangs of hunger for several days that they began to grumble and talk of returning home. But Fronto was indignant. "The Lord will provide," he said. "O ye of little faith!" And he bade them go to work and try to forget their hunger. The monks drew the cords tighter about their waists. But that did little good. They had never fasted like this before! Day by day they grew more pale and thin, and their long robes flapped about their lean limbs. The few dates which grew on

Saints and Friendly Beasts

the palm-trees of their oasis were long since eaten, and the poor monks went about chewing the knotted ends of their rope girdles, trying to pretend that it was bread. Oh, how they longed for even a bit of the hard black bread which was Lenten fare at the monastery beyond the hills!

Day by day they grew more hollow-cheeked and despairing. At last one evening they came to Fronto in a body — such a weak, pale body. "Take us back to Nitria, or we starve!" they cried. "We can endure this no longer!"

Fronto stood before them even more pale and worn than the rest, but with the light of beautiful trust in his eyes. "Wait yet a little longer, brothers," he begged. "We are bidden to take no thought to the morrow, what we shall eat and drink"—

"Nay, 'tis to-day we think of," interrupted the monks. "If we could eat to-day we would indeed take no thought of the morrow. But we starve!"

"Patience, brothers," continued the Saint wearily. "If we return now we shall show that we distrust God's promise. Wait till to-morrow. If help come not then, I give ye leave to go, without me. I shall not return."

The monks withdrew, still grumbling and unhappy. But the words of the Saint had made some impression, and they agreed to wait until morning. Each monk stretched himself on his goatskin mat on the floor of the little cell which he had dug in the sand. And with groans of hunger mingled in their prayers they tried to go to sleep and forget how long it was since their last breakfast.

But Fronto could not sleep. He was sad and disappointed because his brothers had lost their faith, and because he felt alone, deserted in this desert by the friends who should have helped him with their sympathy and trust. All night he knelt on his goatskin mat praying that the Lord would fulfill His promise now, and prove to the doubting monks how mistaken their lack of faith had been. The other monks slept a hungry sleep about him, dreaming of delicious things to eat. Now and then one of them would cry out: "Another help of pudding, please;" or "Brother, will you pass the toast?" or "Thank you, I will have an egg, brother." And Fronto wept as he heard how faint their voices were.

Saint Fronto's Camels

At last the pink fingers of morning began to spread themselves over the face of the sky, pinching its cheeks into a rosy red. Suddenly Fronto, who was on his knees with his back to the door of his cell, started. Hark! what sound was that which came floating on the fresh morning air? Surely, the tinkle of a bell. The good Saint rose from his mat and went hastily to the door, his sure hope sending a smile to his pale lips and color to his hollow cheek. He knew that his prayer was answered. And lo! away in the northwest he saw a thread of black, crawling like a caterpillar over the sand toward his oasis. Nearer and nearer it came; and now he could see plainly what it was, — a line of great rocking camels, the little tinkling bells on whose harness gave the signal that hope was at hand.

But the sound had waked the other monks. With a cry of joy they came tumbling out of their cells and rushed toward the camels, which were now close to the camp. How the poor monks ran, to be sure, many of them tripping over the skirts of their long robes and falling flat in the sand from their weakness and excitement. They were like men on a sinking ship who had just caught sight of a rescuing sail. Some of them jumped up and down and clapped their hands like children, they were so glad. And tears stood in the eyes of nearly all.

There were seventy camels, soft-eyed gentle creatures, whose flat feet held them up on the soft sand like snowshoes. They bore packs upon their backs which promised good things, and they came straight to the cell of Fronto, where they stopped. And what a welcome they received! The monks threw their arms about the beasts' necks, as they knelt on the sand, and kissed the soft noses as though they were greeting long-lost brothers. They were so glad to see the camels themselves that they almost forgot to wonder whence they came, or what they were bringing. But Fronto was looking for their owner, for the man who drove them. There was no one to be found. They had come all alone across the desert, without any one to guide them. Fronto's face was full of joy. "The Lord has sent them!" he said. And the other monks bowed their heads, and were ashamed because they had doubted.

Hungry though they were, first of all the good monks tended the tired beasts who had come so far to save them. They relieved them from their heavy loads, and tenderly washed their hot, weary feet, and gave them draughts of the spring water. Some of the starving monks skurried away to gather the green grass of the oasis for their hungry friends, and others unfastened the bales of hay which some of the camels had brought, and made beds for the animals to lie on. Then they all fell to and built a fold for the seventy camels in the shade of the palm-trees. And here they left the patient creatures to rest and chew their cud with a sigh of relief that the long, hot journey was over.

Then the monks hurried back to Fronto, wondering if it were not now almost time for their breakfast. They came upon him reading a letter which he had found on the harness of the foremost camel. It was written from the city of Alexandria, and it explained how the camels had been sent.

Four nights before this, Glaucus, the rich merchant, had been resting on a couch in his summer house. He had just finished an excellent dinner, with all his favorite fishes and meats and fruits and sweets, and he was feeling very happy. When suddenly he thought of the seventy monks who had gone out from Nitria many days before to live in the desert with the help which the Lord should send. And a pang smote him. Perhaps they were starving now, while he was feasting. And he wished he could help them to a dinner as good as his. Ha! an idea came to him. Why should he not indeed send them a dinner — many dinners? It should be done.

So the next morning he had loaded seventy camels with provisions, five of them with bales of hay for the camels themselves. And taking them to the border of the desert, without driver or any one to guide them, he had sent them out into the sea of sand, the great ships of the desert, to find the right harbor by themselves. For somehow he felt sure that the Lord would guide them safely to the monks. Here the letter of Glaucus ended.

Oh, how good that breakfast tasted to the poor, famished monks! There were all kinds of fruit, — fresh figs and olives and dates, citrons and juicy grapes and yellow pomegranates. There were bread and oil which the monks loved, and nuts and combs of the most delicious golden honey such as it makes one's mouth water to think of. Glaucus had sent them a breakfast fit for a king. And they all sat down on the sand in a happy circle and had the finest picnic that was ever seen in that desert.

When they had eaten they went out once more to visit the camels who had saved their lives, and to thank them with caressing words. The camels seemed to understand, and looked at them with gentle eyes, chewing their cud earnestly as if thinking: "You see, the Lord was looking out for you all the time. We are only poor, dumb beasts; but we came straight to you across the desert without any fear or wandering, because we trusted. Why were you not trustful, too?"

And again the monks were very much ashamed, and went back to Fronto to beg his forgiveness, promising never again to be faint-hearted nor to lose faith.

The next morning they made ready to send back the camels to Alexandria. For they knew Glaucus would be anxious to hear how his ships of the desert had fared on their errand. And half the provisions they returned, for they had more than enough to last them a year, according to their simple meals. Then, with tears in their eyes, the monks sent the great beasts forth again into the desert, confident that as they had come so they would find their way back to Alexandria, safe and sound. Each in his cell door the monks stood and watched them slowly winding away over the yellow sand, disappearing at last behind the hills which rose like great waves between them and the world of cities.

Now it was eight days since Glaucus had sent out the camels, and he was growing uneasy. Seventy camels are a valuable property, which even a rich man could not afford to lose. Glaucus feared that he had been foolish; the desert was full of robbers, and there was no one to protect this leaderless caravan. Would the Lord take care of affairs which were left wholly to His direction?

Glaucus was sitting with his family in the garden, silent and gloomy. His family felt that he had been rash, and they did not hesitate to tell him so, which made him still more unhappy. The leader-camel was the favorite of Glaucus's daughter, Æmilia. She was crying in a corner of the garden, thinking about her dear Humpo, whom she never expected to see again. When, just as Fronto had done, she heard a far-away tinkle. She jumped up and ran out to the road.

"What is it, Æmilia, my child?" called out her father, startled by her sudden movement.

"Oh, Father, Father!" she cried. "I think I hear the tinkle of a camel bell among the mountains!" And sure enough. As they all hurried down to the garden gate the sound of little bells drew nearer and nearer. And presently came in sight the line of seventy camels, Humpo at the head, half of them loaded with the provisions which the monks were too unselfish to keep. And soon Æmilia had her arms about the neck of her dear Humpo, and was whispering nice things into his floppy ears as he knelt before her, looking lovingly at her with his big brown eyes.

Thus it was that Glaucus, the good rich man, knew that the Lord was pleased with him for his kindness, and had helped him to do his duty. And every year after that he sent the seventy camels forth into the desert on their unguided errand to the far-off oasis. So they grew to be dear friends of Saint Fronto and his monks, looked for as eagerly as Santa Claus is at Christmas time.

The Blind Singer Saint Hervé

Once upon a time when Childebert was King of France, a thousand years ago, there lived a young man named Hyvarnion who was very handsome and had the sweetest voice. Hyvarnion was the King's minstrel; he lived at the palace and it was his business to make music for the King to keep him in a good temper. For he wrote the most beautiful songs and sang them to the accompaniment of a golden harp which he carried with him everywhere he went. And besides all this Hyvarnion was very wise; so wise that when he was a boy at school he was called the Little Sage, for Saint Cadoc had been his master and had taught him many things that even the King, who was a heathen, did not know.

Now Hyvarnion had lived four years with the King when one night he had a wonderful dream. He dreamed that he saw a beautiful maiden picking flowers in a meadow, and that she smiled at him and gave him a blossom, saying, "This is for my King." And Hyvarnion woke up longing to see the maiden more than anything else in the world.

For three nights he dreamed the same dream, of the singing maiden and the meadow and the flowers; and each time she seemed more beautiful than on the last. So on the fourth day he woke up and said, "I must find that maiden. I must find her and hear her call me her King."

So, taking his golden harp on his back, he went out from the palace and struck into the deep black forest. By and by he came to an open place, like a meadow, where the grass grew tall and thick, and where in the midst was a spring like a bit of mirror set in a green frame. And Hyvarnion's heart beat fast with joy when he saw on the border of the spring the very maiden about whom he had dreamed, but much more beautiful than any dream. She was bending over, picking something from the grass, and she seemed like a wonderful pink-and-white flower set among the other flowers of yellow and red and blue.

For a moment Hyvarnion stood and gazed with open mouth and

HYVARNION AND RIVANONE

happy eyes. Then he took his harp and began to sing a song which he had just that minute made. For because he was a minstrel it was easier for him to sing than to talk. And in the song he called her

Queen Iris gathering flowers for her crown. Then the maiden raised her head and she turned pinker and whiter, and looked even more like a fair flower than before. For she too had had a dream, three times. And it was of golden-haired Hyvarnion that she had dreamed, whom she now saw looking at her and singing so sweetly with his silver voice.

But she also answered him in a song, for she was a singer, too. "I am no Queen Iris," she sang, "I am only the little maiden Rivanone, though they call me Queen of this Fountain. And I am not gathering flowers as you say, fair Sir, but I am seeking simple herbs such as wise men use to cure pain and trouble."

"What are the herbs you seek, Rivanone?" asked Hyvarnion, coming nearer. She held up a sprig of green in her white hand. "See, this is the vervain," she answered in song; "this brings happiness and heart's ease. But I seek two others which I have not found. The second opens the eyes of the blind. And the third, — few may ever find that precious herb, — the third is the root of life, and at its touch death flees away. Alas!

"Fair Sir, I cannot find those two, though some day I feel that I shall need them both most sorely." Rivanone sighed and two tears stood like dewdrops in her flower eyes.

But Hyvarnion had now come very close. "Still, you have found the first, which gives happiness, little Queen," he sang tenderly. "Have you not happiness to share with me, Rivanone?" Then the maiden looked up in his eyes and smiled, and held out to him a sprig of the green vervain.

"For my King," she sang, just as he had dreamed. And then he did just what she had dreamed he would do; but that is a secret which I cannot tell. For no one knows all that a maiden dreams.

And after this and that they came back to the King's palace hand in hand, singing a beautiful song which, together, they had made about Happiness. So they were married at the court, and the King did them great honor and made them King and Queen of music and of song.

So, happily they lived and happily they sang in their little Kingdom of Poesie, — for did they not possess the herb of joy which Rivanone had found and shared with Hyvarnion, her King?

II.

But it was a pity that Rivanone had not also found those other plants for which she had been seeking, the root which brings light to the blind, and the root which gives life to the dying. Because Rivanone had foreseen only too well the need of them which would come to her. For when, after a year or two, their little son was born, his blue eyes were sightless and all the colored wonders of the world were secrets which he could never know. So they named him Hervé, which means Bitterness, — the first bitterness which had come into their lives of joy. But it was not the last. Not long after the little Hervé came, golden-haired Hyvarnion lay ill and dying. And because on that spring morning, Rivanone had not found the herb of life, she could not keep him from going away to find it for himself in that fair country where it is the only plant that grows, with wonderful blossoms which no living man has ever seen.

So Hyvarnion passed away from his kingdom of music and song, which he left to be shared by dear Rivanone and Hervé his little son. Thus Hervé became a Prince, heir to all the gifts of that royal pair. And of these there were in particular four of the best: a beautiful face, the sweetest voice that ever thrilled in Brittany, the golden harp of Hyvarnion his father, and many a lovely song made by those two, which Rivanone taught him. What a wonderful Kingdom that was to be his! What beautiful gifts for a little boy to own!

But even in a kingdom of this sort one has to bear sorrows and discomforts, just as folk do in other kingdoms which are less fair. Hervé's name meant bitterness, and there was much bitterness in his little life before he learned what a Prince he really was. For he was blind and could not play with the other children. Rivanone was a poor widow and there was no one to earn bread for the two. Sometimes the carols which they sang together were the only breakfast to begin the day. Sometimes the songs Rivanone made beside his bed at night were the only food Hervé had tasted since sunrise. Sometimes they were both so hungry that they could not sing at all; and those were sad times indeed.

But when Hervé was seven years old a great idea came to him. Rivanone lay ill and miserable, and there was nothing to eat in the house. Hervé sat by her side holding her hand, and wishing there was something he could do about it. Blind as he was he had never been out of the house alone. But suddenly courage came to him and hope, through his great idea.

"I will save you, dear mother!" he cried, throwing his arms about her neck. "I will take father's golden harp and go out upon the highway and sing your beautiful songs. People will give me pennies, and I shall buy you food."

So, carrying the golden harp on his back, in his ragged clothes and bare feet the little fellow went out stumbling and feeling his way along the hard road. Now almost at the first corner he met a white dog, who seemed to have no master. This creature came sniffing and whining up to Hervé and licked his hand. And when the boy went on the dog followed close at his side as if to guide and protect him. Hervé asked every one he met whose dog it was; but they all said it was a strange dog come from Nowhere, and belonged to No-one. It seemed almost as if the beast had been sent especially for Hervé. So at last he said, "You shall be my dog," and at that the great white beast jumped up and barked for joy. Hervé fastened a rope about the dog's neck and kept one end in his hand. So now he had some one to guide and guard him, for the dog was very careful and kind and took care that Hervé never stumbled nor went astray into the ditch by the side of the road.

It must have been a hard-hearted man indeed who had no pennies to spare for the blind boy led by the big white dog. With his bare feet blue with cold, his teeth chattering, and his eyes turned wistfully up to the sky which he could not see, he was a sad little figure to meet on the lonely Brittany roads. And he sang so sweetly, too! No one had ever heard such a voice as that, nor such beautiful songs. Every one who heard gave him money. So he was helping his mother, getting her food and medicine and clothes to keep her warm. And this thought comforted him when he was shivering with cold, his rags blown about by the wind and soaked in the rain.

Day after day, week after week, Hervé trudged along the flinty roads. Often he limped with cold, bleeding feet which the faithful dog would try to lick warm again. Often he was very tired, and sometimes he was sad, when people were not kind. But this seldom happened.

Saints and Friendly Beasts

Once Hervé was passing through a strange village where all the folk were heathen. And a band of naughty children began to dance about him and tease him, pulling his hair and twitching his cloak. And they mocked his music, singing, "Blind boy, blind boy! Where are you going, blind boy!" Then it is said that a wonderful thing happened. Hervé was sorry because they were so cruel and unkind, and he struck a strange chord of music on his harp and sang in a low, clear voice, —

"Dance on, bright eyes who can see. Dance on, children who mock a poor blind boy. Dance on, — and never stop so long as the world wags." And it is said that the wicked children are still dancing, over the world and back, around and around, tired though they must be. And they will be still more tired before all is done. For they must whirl and pirouette until the end of the world; and that is a long time even for children who love to dance.

At a different time another unkind thing happened to Saint Hervé. But this time it was a beast who hurt his feelings. And this was strange; for usually the beasts loved him and tried to help him as the white dog had done. But after all this was only a mistake; yet it was a sad mistake, for it cost Hervé the life of his faithful guide. This is how it happened.

As Hervé and his dog were passing along a lonely road, a black wolf sprang out upon them. He mistook the dog for an ancient enemy of his, another wolf. For indeed Blanco looked like a white wolf, — a wolf such as Saint Bridget gave the King of Ireland. And without stopping to find out who he really was, which would have saved all the trouble, they had a terrible fight, and poor Blanco was killed by the huge black wolf.

Then Hervé was sad indeed. He cried and sobbed and was so wretched that the wolf was sorry. Besides, as soon as the fight was over the wolf had found out his mistake, and saw that it was a strange dog whom he had killed, no wolf-enemy at all. He was very much ashamed. He came up to Hervé and fawned at his feet, trying to tell that he was sorry, and asking what he should do about it So Hervé told him that if he would be his dog now instead of Blanco he would try to forgive the wolf; though he was, oh, so sorry to lose his faithful dog.

The Blind Singer Saint Hervé

After that Hervé went on his wanderings led by a big black wolf whom he held in a strong leather leash. And the wolf became as dear to him as Blanco had been. He slept in the barn with the oxen when he was at home, and never snapped nor bit at them as most wolves would do. But he kept sharp watch over his little master, and saw that no one hurt or cheated him. I should be sorry to think what would have happened to any one who had dared to touch Hervé while the wolf was near. And he was always near, with his sharp teeth and watchful eyes.

So they wandered and wandered together, Hervé and the wolf, carrying music from town to town, the songs of Hyvarnion and Rivanone. But Hervé had not yet learned to make songs of his own.

III.

Now after seven years of wandering, Hervé had earned money enough to keep his mother in comfort. He longed to go to school and be taught things, to grow wise like his father, who had been called the Little Sage, and to learn how to make songs for himself. For he felt that it was time for him to come into the kingdom of Hyvarnion and Rivanone; and the songs shut in his heart were bursting to come out.

Gourvoyed, the brother of Rivanone, was a holy hermit who lived alone in the forest, and he would teach Hervé, his nephew, for love of him. For Gourvoyed was a wise man, skilled in all things, but especially in the making of songs.

It was a blessed morning when Hervé started for his school in the woods; he was going to his kingdom! The sunlight framed his fair curls in a halo of light, as if giving him a blessing. Birds sang all along the way as if telling him that with Gourvoyed he would learn to make music even sweeter than theirs. The wolf led him eagerly, bounding with joy; for he shared in all the hopes of Hervé's life. And all the creatures knew that he would become a great poet. And so indeed it was.

For Hervé soon learned all that Gourvoyed could teach, and in his turn he became a master. Many pupils came to the hut in the forest which the hermit gave up to him, and begged Hervé to make them singer-poets like himself. But he could not do that. He could teach them to sing and to play the harp; but no one could sing as well as he sang, or play as well as he played. And no one can ever be taught to make poetry unless he has it in his soul, as Hervé had. For that is a royal gift, and it came to Hervé from Hyvarnion and Rivanone, the King and Queen of music and of song. It was Hervé's kingdom, and it was given him to take away the bitterness from his name, to make it remembered as sweet, sweet, sweet.

And now on his wanderings from town to town Hervé was received like a prince. He sat at great lords' tables, and sang in ladies' bowers. He had golden goblets as his gifts, and shining gems to wear if he chose. But he was so generous that he gave them all away. Never was there heard music so sweet as his; never were there songs so beautiful as he sang to the rippling of his father's golden harp. For Hervé was even a greater minstrel than Hyvarnion or Rivanone had been.

In his wanderings all about the country Hervé came to many strange places and met with many strange adventures. Once he spent the night at the castle of a great lord who made Hervé sit on his right hand at table and honored him above all his guests. When the banquet was over, at the Count's request a page brought to Hervé his golden harp, and they all shouted for "A song! a song!" Every one pushed back his stool to listen, and Hervé took the harp and ran his finger over the golden strings with a sound like drops of rain upon the flowers.

Now outside the castle, beyond the moat, was a pond. And in the pond lived a whole colony of great green bullfrogs, whose voices were gruffer and grummer than the lowest twanging note on Hervé's harp. And as soon as Hervé began to sing these rude frogs began to bellow and growl as if trying to drown his music. Perhaps they were jealous; for Hervé's voice was sweeter than a silver bell. But all they could sing was "Ker-*chog*! Ker-r-kity-chog, Ker-*chog*!" which is neither very musical nor very original, being the same tune which all the frog-people have sung from the earliest days.

Now Hervé was displeased by their disagreeable noise. He could not sing nor play, nor think of the words which belonged with his music: only the "Ker-chog! Ker-r-kity-chog! Ker-chog!" sounded in his ears. And it grew louder and louder every moment as one by one all the frogs joined in the chorus.

Hervé waited for them to stop. But when he found that they did not mean to do this, but were really trying to drown his voice, he was very angry. He strode to the window holding his harp in his hand. And leaning far out he struck another of his wonderful chords of music, such as had charmed the mocking children once before, as you remember.

"Sing your last song, O Frogs," he said. "Sing your last Ker-chog, for henceforth you will be silent. I command you from this night never to open your mouths again. All save one, the littlest of you all. And he shall sing forever, without cease, to remind you of your rudeness to me." And no sooner had he ceased speaking when there came a great silence outside the window, broken only by one wee piping tadpole voice. "Ker-chog! Ker-r-kity-chog! Ker-chog!" he chanted his sad little solo. And all alone he had to sing and sing this same tune forever. I dare say one can hear him yet in the greeny pond outside that old French castle.

IV.

Now after many years of wandering, of singing, of making beautiful songs, of teaching and wandering again, Hervé's dear mother Rivanone died. But he still had some one to love and look for him and the wolf when he came home from his travels. For Rivanone had adopted a dear little girl named Christine, beautiful as sunshine and sweet as a flower. She called Hervé "Uncle" and loved him dearly, and the wolf was a great friend of hers.

So at last he thought to settle down and make music about him in his own home, letting people come there to hear it, instead of carrying it to them by road and river. For he was growing an old man, and it was not so easy to travel in his blindness as it used to be. Besides, the black wolf was also growing gray, and needed rest after these long years of faithful work.

Hervé resolved to build a church, and to live there with Christine near him in a little house of her own. He had grown to be an important personage in the world, and had many friends, pupils, and followers who wanted to live near him. So forth they set to find a place for their church, Hervé and his troop of black-robed monks. And before them, like a little white dove among the ravens, ran Christine holding her uncle's hand in one of hers, and in the other grasping the leash at which tugged the grizzled old wolf who was guiding them. Over many a hill and dale and bloomy meadow he had led Hervé before now, down many a lane and village street, but never upon so important a journey as this. For this was to be the old wolf's last long tramp with his master. And the wolf was to choose the spot where the church should stand. Where he stopped to rest, there would they lay the first stone.

So he led them on and on. And at last he lay down in a green spot by a river, just the place for a beautiful church to grow up. And thenceforth Hervé the minstrel would wander no more, but bide and rest and be happy with the wolf and Christine.

They built her an arbor near the church, in a clump of willows on the border of a spring. It was cone-shaped and covered with straw like a huge beehive. And Christine herself seemed like a busy bee gathering honey as she buzzed in and out among the roses, humming little tunes below her breath. For she was always among the flowers, as Rivanone had been. Every Saturday morning she would rise early, and with her little basket on her arm would go out to pick the blossoms with the dew still on them. And every Saturday evening she came to the church with her arms full of flowers till she looked like a bouquet of sweetness. And going into the empty church she would busy herself with arranging the flowers for the next morning's service. For it was her duty to see that Uncle Hervé's church was kept clean and sweet and beautiful.

And while Christine stood there putting the flowers into tall golden vases, singing softly the songs which Rivanone had taught her, her Uncle Hervé would come creeping up the steps of the church, his hand on the head of the wolf, who always led him to the place where he heard her voice. Softly, very softly, as if he were doing something naughty, Hervé would pull open the heavy door, just a crack, the better to hear her sing. Then he would put his ear to the opening; while the wolf would thrust his nose in below, and wag his tail eagerly. But Christine's keen ears always heard them, no matter how slyly the good blind man crept up to that door. And it became part of the game that she should cry out suddenly, —

"I see you, Uncle! I see you!" And though he could not see her at all, he would start and pop back, pulling the wolf with him as though he had done something wrong. Then without making any noise they would tiptoe away to Hervé's house, their hearts beating with love for the dear little maiden who would soon come to bid them good-night on her way home to her bower.

So they lived happily all the rest of their days, these three among the flowers. And in spite of his name Hervé's life was not one of bitterness, but of joy. The kingdom which had come to him from Hyvarnion and Rivanone was his all his life long; and though he no longer wandered painfully from town to town, the songs which he made wandered still from heart to heart. And long, long afterwards their echo made music through the land of Brittany, as the fragrance of a flower lasts long after the flower has passed on its way elsewhere.

Dear Saint Hervé!

Saint Comgall and the Mice

At the place where the Irish Sea is narrowest is the town of Bangor. There the green hills of Saint Patrick's island smile over at the purple cliffs of Scotland across the lane of water where the ships pass to and fro, just as neighbors nod across a narrow street above the heads of the passers-by. And here at Bangor Saint Comgall built a monastery, thirteen hundred long years ago.

This does not sound very interesting, but it was interesting to many people in those days, and I think it will be interesting to you. For Comgall is an Irish word which means "the goodly pledge." And the man who bore this name was a goodly pledge of friendship between man and beast. Comgall had many pupils in his monastery, and many friends living near who loved and honored him. They did splendid things together, and tales of their doings were put into great books. But the most interesting stories of all are about certain friends of Saint Comgall who could not speak Irish and who did not wear clothes. Some of these friends wore feathers and some wore fur; the strangest story of all is about his friends with long tails and very sharp teeth. But you must wait for that till I have told about the swans.

One day Comgall was walking with some friends on the bank of a pond. All of a sudden, through the rushes and the tall grass some one spied six beautiful white swans floating on the water, preening their fine feathers and arching their necks proudly. For they could see in the water, just as if it were a mirror, how handsome they were, and it made them vain.

"Oh, Father," cried Comgall's pupils (they always called their teacher "Father" in those days), "see the lovely swans! May we not coax them ashore? We want to play with them."

Comgall chuckled inside, for he felt sure that the swans would not come to them, because they were strangers. But he said with a twinkle in his eye, —

"Oh, yes, boys. Call them here if you can. But you must give them something to tempt them, or I fear they will hardly come."

Then the boys tried to find a crust of bread or some crumbs in their pockets, to throw to the swans. But no one had anything, not even a peanut; for peanuts were not invented in those days. They stood on the bank whistling and calling, trying in every way to make the swans swim ashore. But the birds only cocked their red-rimmed eyes at the boys and fluttered their wings timidly.

"We don't know you," they squawked with their harsh voices. "The like of you are no friends of ours. Hurrooh! Go away and leave our pond in peace."

All this time Comgall had been standing behind them on the bank laughing at the vain attempts of his pupils. But now he walked quietly down to the pond. Making a little croony sound in his throat, he put out his hand towards the swans, but with no crumbs to tempt them.

The swans had never before seen him. But as soon as they heard his voice you should have seen the commotion! How the water did wrinkle and spatter as those dignified birds scurried headlong towards Comgall! Each one seemed trying to be the first to reach his side; and each one flapped his wings and went almost into a fit for fear another should get ahead of him. So finally they reached the bank and gathered around Comgall, talking to him all at once and telling him how much they liked the look of him. And one great white swan fluttered into the old man's lap and sat there letting himself be stroked and patted, stretching his long neck up to Comgall's face and trying to kiss him with beaky lips.

You can imagine how the pupils stared at this strange sight. For they knew that the swans were as truly strangers to Saint Comgall as to the rest of them. But the swans had guessed in some way that this was a man who loved all animals, and that is why they were not afraid, but loved him as soon as they saw him.

But this next is the stranger story. Mice are harder even than swans for most people to get acquainted with. But Comgall had also made the mice his friends, as you shall see.

There came a time of famine in Ireland, and there was not food enough to go around, as has often happened there from the earliest days until even now. Comgall and his household at Bangor were very hungry. But what made it hardest to bear was that they knew where there was plenty of food close by, if only they could get it. For Croadh

Saint Comgall and the Mice

was a great Prince who lived in the neighborhood, and Croadh had barns and storehouses full of grain which could be made into bread. But he was a selfish, stingy man and would not give away or even sell his stores, for he would rather see the people starve. Now Croadh had a wicked old mother living in his palace, who was even more cruel than himself. Her name was Luch, and Luch means in Irish "the Mouse." And it was her name which put an idea into Comgall's head.

After sending all sorts of messengers to beg Croadh to give them some of his grain; after trying all sorts of ways to make him sell it, Comgall went himself to the Prince's palace to see what he could do. He carried with him a beautiful silver goblet which had been given him by some one as a present, and it was worth many bushels of grain.

Comgall strode into the Prince's hall and stood before Croadh holding out the goblet in his hand. And he said, —

"Here, O Prince, is a valuable thing. We are starving in the monastery, and silver we cannot eat. Give me and my monks some of your golden grain and I will exchange for it the silver cup. Be merciful, O Croadh, and hear me."

But the Chief only laughed and said mockingly, "Not so. You keep your silver goblet and I will keep my golden grain. Your beggarly pupils shall not eat of my stores. I want all, every grain, for my old Mouse." And by that word he meant his mother, the black-eyed, wrinkled, gray old Luch, whose name meant "the Mouse." For she was the most miserly, wicked, old woman in the world, and she had made him promise not to give up any of the grain. Then Comgall was angry, because he saw that the Prince meant to see the people starve.

"Very well," he said, fixing his eyes sternly upon Croadh, "as you have said, so shall it be. The mouse shall have your grain." And drawing his robe about him he strode home with the useless silver goblet.

As I have said, the mice were Comgall's friends. He had only to call them and explain what the hard-hearted Prince had done; he had only to tell the mice what he wished them to do, and the matter was settled. The word spread through the kingdom of the mice, carried by the quickest messenger with the shortest tail. All the mice became enemies of Croadh. And there were many mice in Bangor in those days. That very night when every one was asleep, out of every hole and corner came peeping little pointed noses and quivering whiskers. And a great procession of long-tailed tiny things formed into line and crept along, and along, up the hill, and up the walls, and into the barns of Croadh. A legion of mice, thousands upon thousands of them in a gray-uniformed army, pounced upon the Prince's precious grain and ate up every kernel.

So the next morning when Croadh went to his barns he found them empty. There was not so much as a single yellow dot of grain left anywhere. But out of every crack and crevice peeped a pair of twinkling black eyes which watched him saucily. Then Croadh began to bellow and roar with anger, and the wicked old woman Luch, his mother, came hobbling in to see what was the matter. But when the mice saw her they gave a chorus of fierce squeaks as if crying "Mouse! Mouse! Mouse!"

Then Croadh remembered what Comgall had said, that the mouse should have his grain after all. And he guessed what the Saint had meant, and knew that Comgall had taken this way to punish a selfish and cruel man.

The Wonders of Saint Berach

The life of Saint Berach was full of wonders from the very first. For when he was a boy at home in the house of his father, Nemnald, he had a vision. An angel appeared to him and beckoned him to follow. So he went, and the angel led him straight to the monastery at Glendalough where holy Saint Cœmgen lived with his friend the white doe, and taught boys to be wise. And Berach joined the other boys to be taught all that Saint Cœmgen knew, and to learn other things beside.

Ireland was a wild country in those days, for this was only six hundred years after Christ's birth and the little towns had hardly begun to grow. The huts which men had made in the wilderness — calling them houses and schools and churches — were not close together but far, far apart. Wild beasts prowled everywhere, and there were no policemen.

Close by the monastery were the broad green meadows where the monks pastured the herds of cows which gave them milk. From the windows of his cell the young monk loved to watch the cows and their calves browsing the juicy grass and wading in the brooks which ran under the rows of willows. He especially loved Bel, the sleekest, most beautiful of them all, a proud mother cow who had a new little red calf.

One day as he was watching Bel and her baby who had strayed a little distance from the rest of the herd, he saw something which frightened him. A great gray wolf was hiding in the shadow of a hedge, creeping nearer and nearer to the peaceful pair. But Bel did not guess that an enemy was so near. Berach hurried down the turret stair and out of the gate, hardly pausing to tell the brother porter whither he was going. For he knew there was no time to lose.

He ran to the meadow, and pushed through the blooming hedge of hawthorn. But alas! he had come too late. The great gaunt wolf, who was very hungry, had pounced upon the little red calf, and had eaten it up. Poor Bel, wild with grief, ran lowing about the pasture as if seeking for her little one. But the wolf was slinking out of sight.

Saints and Friendly Beasts

When Berach saw what had been done, at first he was very angry with the wolf, for he loved Bel dearly, and it troubled him to see her sad. He thought how lonely the poor cow would be without her calf, and when she came pitifully lowing up to him as if asking him to help her, the tears stood in his kind eyes. But then he thought how hungry the wolf must have been. Poor thing, how thin and hollow he had looked, — perhaps he was not so much to blame after all. Probably he had never been taught any better.

And then a strange idea came to Berach. He was a wonderful man, and he must have had great power over animals. For he called to the wolf, who was already some distance away; he called loudly and in a stern voice. You will hardly believe it, but the wolf came slinking back, frightened and whining like a naughty puppy, and crouched at Berach's feet. Then the Saint spoke kindly to the wolf, no longer treating him like a murderer and a thief. He called the cow also, and taking her by the horns led her gently to the wolf, soothing her so that she was not afraid of the great gray beast.

And Berach said to the cow, "See, Mother Bel, this shall be your child now, in place of the little one which is gone. He will be a kind and gentle son to you, I promise." And to the wolf he said, "Here, Wolf, is the mother whom you need to make you gentle and good. You shall be kind to her, and make her forget the wrong you have done by being a loving and dutiful son, ever doing her bidding." So after that the cow and the meek wolf dwelt peacefully together in the meadows of the monastery, and he shielded her from danger, and like a huge watchdog kept away the other wild beasts from the herd.

After that came a winter when for weeks the ground was white with snow, and the laughing mouths of the brooks were sealed with ice. Duke Colman's little son had been sent to school at the monastery, and the boy was very ill. He was hot and thirsty, and his throat was parched with fever. So little Edward begged for juicy apples, and for salad of fresh sorrel leaves, — things which were not to be found in all the land in the dead of winter. But Cœmgen the Abbot trusted in the power of his young friend who could tame wolves. "Go forth, my son," he said to Berach, "take my staff and bring what the boy needs."

Then Berach retired to his cell and prayed that he might be blessed to save the dear child's life. After that with faith and courage

The Wonders of Saint Berach

he went out into the white meadows, using the Abbot's staff to help him over the great drifts of snow. He came to the row of willows by the frozen brook where the cows had loved to wade. And here he paused. Lifting the staff, he touched the bare brown branches of the willow on which the snow clung like shreds of cotton wool, and he pronounced a blessing. Instantly the snow began to melt as it does before the sun in April. The stiff brown twigs turned green and became tender and full of life. Then gray willow buds put forth woolly little pussy-willows, which seemed fairly bursting, like fat round kittens. They grew bigger and bigger, rounder and rounder, till at last they really did burst, and plumped great rosy-cheeked apples into the lap of the Saint, who held up the skirt of his gray gown to catch them as they fell. Lo, under the trees meanwhile the snowdrifts had melted, and little green leaves were poking up through the frozen ground. And Berach gathered there a great bunch of juicy, tart sorrel which makes such good salad. Then with his arms full, — what with this and his apples and the blessed staff, — he floundered back through the snowdrifts to the monastery. They received him eagerly and there was great rejoicing. Little Edward was revived by the out-of-season dainties thus miraculously provided for him, and soon became quite well again.

It was many years after this, again a hard and cruel winter, when Saint Berach made another wonder come to pass. Meantime he had grown older and even wiser. He had himself been made Abbot and had built a monastery of his own in a lonely place far away from Glendalough. But he had an enemy. There was a rich man who wanted the land which Berach had chosen, and who was so envious that he tried to do him spite in every way he could. He even sought to destroy the monastery. Then Berach appealed to the King for protection, and both men were summoned to the court.

The rich man went in a chariot, splendid in his fine robes of fur, with a gold chain about his neck. And the guards hurried to let down the portcullis for him, and with low bows bade him enter. But when Saint Berach came he wore only his gray monk's robe, all torn and tattered. He was shivering with cold, and weak from having walked so far. So they thought him a mere beggar and would not let him in. As he stood outside the gate, friendless and alone, some rude boys who had gathered there began to laugh and jeer at his bare sandaled feet and the rents in his robe through which the cold winds blew. They made snowballs and rushed upon him in a crowd, like the cowards they were, pelting the poor man most cruelly. But suddenly, what do you think? Their arms stiffened as they raised them to throw the balls; their legs stuck fast in the snow; the grins froze on their faces; and they were almost choked by the shouts which turned to ice in their throats. What had happened? Well, Saint Berach had merely breathed upon them, and they were as if turned into ice, so that they could not stir. Br-r-r! How cold they were!

Then the Saint made ready to warm himself. A drift of snow had fallen from the palace gate when it opened to let in the rich man. And going up to this he blew upon it. He blew a warm breath this time. Instantly the whole heap burst into flame, and snapped and crackled like the fire in the chimney-place of the dining-hall at home. In front of this merry blaze the good Saint stood, warming his hands and thawing out his poor frozen feet. But the group of boys stood like statues of snow; so cold, so cold, but unable to come nearer to the fire; so frightened, so frightened, but unable to run away.

This is what the King's guards saw when, terrified by the crackling of the fire and the great light which shone through the chinks of the gate, they came to see what it all meant. They ran to the King and told him of the strange sight. And he himself with a crowd of courtiers came out to look. When he saw the ragged beggar who had done all this he was filled with amazement. He immediately suspected that this must be a holy man and powerful. So he invited Berach into the palace hall, and there listened to his story.

Now when all was done the rich man was bundled away in disgrace, for daring to meddle with the good works of so wonderful a Saint. But Berach was honored and admired.

Before he went back to his monastery they begged him to restore the naughty boys to life and motion. Now Berach had wanted only to teach them a lesson, not to punish them too severely; for he was too kind-hearted to injure any living creature. So going out into the courtyard he blew upon the snow figures, and once more they became live boys. You can imagine how glad they were when they found they were able to move their legs and arms again.

The Wonders of Saint Berach

Now Berach went back to his monastery in one of the King's chariots, with a robe of fur and a gold chain about his neck. And you may be sure he carried with him many other gifts and precious things from the King, who never thereafter suffered him to be troubled in his far-off retreat.

Saint Prisca, The Child Martyr

Saint Prisca's name has always been dearly loved, especially in England. January eighteenth is the day which is sacred to her, and she lived over seventeen hundred years ago. She is one of the few child-martyrs whose names have come down to us from those early days, although there were many other brave children who suffered and were strong, and who, at last, gave their lives to prove their faith.

Saint Prisca was a little Roman girl whose parents were Christians of a noble family. Claudius was the Emperor at that time, and though during his reign the Christians were not persecuted in such numbers as they had been before that, still many cruel things were done here and there, and it was a dangerous thing to be a Christian.

It was in the evil times when one did not always dare to say what he really thought, nor publicly to worship as he believed was right. Many of the Christians were not ashamed to conceal their real belief from the heathen Romans, who were everywhere seeking with hatred for the followers of Christ, to torture and slay them.

Prisca's father and mother had managed to keep their secret, and were not suspected of being Christians. They probably went to church in the secret chapels which the Christians had dug deep in the ground under the city. In these dark, gloomy catacombs, as they were called, the Christians held services directly under the feet of the cruel Romans, who were passing overhead without suspecting what was going on so near to them.

But Prisca scorned to use any precaution. Small and defenseless though she was, she did not fear to tell every one what she believed and Whose Cross she followed. So she soon became known as a firm little Christian maiden. And there were people in the city cruel enough and wicked enough to hate even a little child-Christian and to wish her evil.

These persons reported to the Emperor's officers her brave words of faith, and told them how she would not sacrifice to the Roman gods as the other children did. So very soon she was seized by the guards and brought before the Emperor.

Claudius looked at the little maid in surprise to find her so young. And he thought; "Ho! I shall easily make this small Christian change her mind and obey me." And he bade his men take her to the temple of Apollo and make her offer incense to the beautiful god of the silver bow. So they carried her to the top of the Palatine, one of the seven hills on which Rome was built.

They first passed under a great marble arch and came into a fair courtyard surrounded by fifty-two marble pillars. In the centre of this space stood the temple of Apollo, the most magnificent building in all Rome. With its ivory gates and wonderful groups of statues, its inlaid marble floors and altars wreathed with flowers, its golden tripods breathing incense, its lamps and beautiful silver vases, it was a very different place from the bare, dark caverns in which the Christians worshiped. In front of the temple was a group of four oxen made of bronze, and in the centre of this group burned a fire upon a golden tripod. This was the altar to Apollo, the sun-god, whose enormous golden statue, in his four-horse chariot, stood over the door of the temple just above. He was the likeness of a beautiful youth with a wreath of bay about his head, carrying a bow in his hand, with which Apollo was believed to shoot the sunbeams down upon the earth.

They thrust incense into Prisca's hand and bade her throw a few grains into the fire in honor of the beautiful god of the sun. It seemed a very simple thing to do, to save her life, — just to scatter a handful of dark powder on the flames. Prisca loved the dear sun as well as any one, but she knew it was foolish to believe that he was a god, and wicked to worship his statue in place of the great God who made the sun and everything else. So Prisca refused to burn the incense.

Then the Emperor was very angry, and bade the soldiers whip her until she obeyed his command. But they could not make her yield by cruelty. Even the hard-hearted Romans who had come to look on admired her bravery and pitied her suffering. The women wept to see her so cruelly treated, and the men cried, "Shame! shame! to torture a little child."

And then a beautiful thing happened; for Prisca appeared dressed in a robe of yellow sunshine. A wonderful light shone all about her, and she seemed herself a little star giving out light, so brightly did

Saint Prisca, The Child Martyr

SAINT PRISCA

her brave spirit shine among those cruel men.

It seemed as if no child could bear all this suffering without yielding, and the Emperor hoped she would give in, for he did not want to have her killed. But Prisca was firm, and would not make the sacrifice. The Emperor was surprised to find a child so brave. He ordered them to drag her away to prison and to keep her there for many days. Here she was most unhappy, — lonely and cold and hungry often, wondering what dreadful thing was to happen next. But her heart was always brave, and she was not afraid.

After a long time, one morning the guard came for little Prisca. They led her forth into the dear sunshine, and glad she was to see it and the blue sky once more. But it was only for a short time that they let her enjoy even this little pleasure; for they brought her to the amphitheatre, a great open place like the circus, with tiers upon tiers of seats all about, and crowds of faces looking down into the centre where she was.

Prisca knew what this meant, for she had often heard how the Christians were put into the arena to be torn in pieces by wild beasts. And kneeling down on the sand she made a little prayer, not that she might be saved from the fierce beasts, but that she might have courage to show her Christian bravery and teach a lesson to these fiercer men and women who were looking on.

Then the keeper opened the grated door of a den at the end of the arena, and out stalked a great yellow lion. With a dreadful roar he rushed into the centre of the circle, and stood there lashing his tail and flashing his big yellow eyes all about the place. Then suddenly he spied the little girl standing quietly at one side with her hands clasped in front of her, looking at him without fear. And the great beast strode gently up to her on his padded paws. He bent his head and licked her little bare feet, and then he crouched down by her side, as a Saint Bernard dog might place himself to guard his little mistress. And this is why the old pictures of Saint Prisca represent her with a lion by her side.

There fell a great silence on the tented place. The Emperor and all the people sat perfectly still, wondering at the strange sight and admiring the courage of the child; for she had reached out her hand and was stroking the yellow head of the lion, playing with his mane. She bent her head and no one heard her whisper into his ear: —

"My good friend! you will not hurt me, I know, for the Lord has closed your mouth, just as he did the mouths of the lions into whose den Daniel was thrown by wicked men. These cruel men will put me to death, but you are kinder than they."

And the lion looked up in her face as though he understood, and growled softly. He was quite gentle with her, but when the keeper came towards them he roared and bristled and showed his great teeth, so that for a long time no one dared to come near.

But even the lion could not save her from the death which she had no wish to shun. At last they captured him and took him away. The Emperor's heart was softened by Prisca's bravery, and he wished to give her one more chance to save her life. They shut her up for many days in the heathen temple, and tried in every way to make her sacrifice to the gods and give up Christianity. They coaxed her and made her fine promises; they threatened and punished her. But still Prisca stood firm, although she was now very worn and tired and ill because she had suffered so much.

So when she had borne it all patiently and bravely, and they saw it was impossible to make a little Christian turn back again into a little heathen, they led her away down the road which leads south from the Palatine hill, to the place of execution. This was just outside the Ostian gate, an archway in the great wall which surrounded Rome, through which the road led to the town of Ostium and to the sea. Just outside this gate, to show that they were no longer worthy of being Romans and living within its walls, criminals were executed. And here many Christian martyrs lost their lives. Prisca was one of these, for here she was beheaded. And till the very end she neither cried nor screamed nor was in any way afraid. And so she became Saint Prisca, a little martyr.

Then another strange thing befell. When she died a great eagle appeared in the sky, hovering over Saint Prisca's body far up in the air. And when any of the Romans ventured near her the eagle swooped down upon them with dreadful cries and flapping of his wings. And his round gray eyes looked so fierce and his claws so long and sharp, that no one dared to touch her for fear of the bird. Saint Prisca had found another protector in cruel Rome. And this is why many of the old pictures of Saint Prisca's martyrdom show a great eagle hovering over her.

The creature guarded her body night and day, driving every one away, until the Christians, who had been waiting for the chance to venture out, came secretly one night and carried her away. They buried her where the Romans could not find her, in their little secret cemetery in the catacombs. This is how Saint Prisca lived and died two hundred and seventy years after Christ's birth. But I wish we knew what became of the noble lion and the devoted eagle.

The Fish Who Helped Saint Gudwall

The Welsh coast is famous for its beautiful scenery and its terrible storms. People who see it in the summer time think only of the beautiful scenery. But if they should happen to pass that way in midwinter they would be very apt to meet an unpleasant reminder of the terrible storms.

Saint Gudwall was born a Welshman, and he should have known all this. Perhaps he did know, but chose to run into danger just because it was dangerous, as so many saints loved to do in those years when it was thought no virtue to take care of one's life. At all events, it was summer when with one friend Gudwall moved to his new home, a tiny island off the coast of Wales, which at that time was very beautiful.

The first thing they did was to set about finding a place to live in. The island was one of those high mountains poking up out of the sea, with green grass on top, like colored frosting to a cake; and gray rocks below, all hollowed out into deep caves and crannies, as if mice had been nibbling at the cake. These caves are just the sort of places which smugglers and pirates choose to hide in with their treasures, for no one would think of hunting for any one there. And Gudwall wanted to be left alone with his pupil; so he thought there was no reason why a bad man's hiding-place should not make a good saint's retreat. So they chose the largest and deepest of all the caves, and there they put their books and their beds and their little furniture, and set up housekeeping.

Their home was one of those caves into which the sea rushes a little way and then suddenly backs out again as if it had changed its mind this time but would call again. Gudwall and his pupil loved to lie in their cave just beyond the reach of the waves and watch them dash laughingly up on the rocks, then roar and gurgle in pretended anger and creep away out into the blue basin beyond. In summer their daily games with the sea were great fun, and Gudwall was very happy. They spent some lovely months alone with the waves and the rocks and the sea-birds which now and then fluttered screaming into the dark cave, and then again dashed bashfully out when they found they had come uninvited into a stranger's home. It was all very nice and peaceful and pretty in the summer time, just as tourists find it to this day.

But oh! what a change when old Winter came roaring down over the waves from the North in his chariot of ice, drawn by fierce winds and angry storm-clouds. Then the temper of the sea was changed. It grew cruel and hungry. It left off its kindly game with the lonely dwellers on the island, and seemed instead to have become their enemy. It tried to seize and swallow them in its cruel jaws.

One morning there came a terrible storm. In the far end of the cave Gudwall and the other were nearly swept away by a huge wave which rushed in to devour them. No longer content with pausing on the threshold, the sea swept through their whole house, dashing away their little store of books and furniture, a most unneighborly thing to do.

It tried to drag the two men from the corner where they clung to the rough rock. Choked and gasping they escaped this time, while the sea drew back for another plunge. But they did not wait for this, for they knew it would mean their death.

Drenched as they were and blinded by the salt spray, they scrambled out of the cave and began to climb the slippery seaweed to the rocks above. It was a hard and dangerous ascent, for the sea leaped after them to pull them back, snarling angrily at their heels like a fierce beast maddened by their escape. But it could not quite seize them, and at last they reached the top of the cliff where they were safe for the time.

But what were they to do now? There were no houses on the island, no place to go to keep warm; yet they could not live out in the open air to freeze in the snow and cold. It was no longer possible to live in the cave if the sea was to wash through it like this. But if only there were some barrier to keep out the stormy waves they could still live in their beloved cave. Saint Gudwall fell upon his knees and prayed for help, — prayed for some defense against the winter waves.

And what do you think happened? The dwellers in the sea were kinder than the sea itself. The little fish who live safely in the angriest

The Fish Who Helped Saint Gudwall

waves were sorry for the big men who were so powerless in the face of this danger. From the sea caves far under the island's foot, from the beds of seaweed and the groves of coral, from the sandy bottom of the ocean fathoms deep below, the fish came swimming in great shoals about Gudwall's island. And each one bore in his mouth a grain of sand. They swam into the shallow water just outside the cave where Gudwall had lived, and one by one they placed their burdens on the sandy bottom. One by one they paused to see that it was well done, then swiftly swam away, to return as soon as might be with another grain of sand. All day long a procession of fish, like people in line at a ticket office, moved steadily up to the shallows and back again. So by night a little bar of sand had begun to grow gradually before the entrance to the cave.

Now Saint Gudwall and his pupil were shivering on the top of the cliff, and looking off to sea, when the pupil caught his master's arm. "What is that down there in the water?" he said, pointing to a little brown spot peering above the waves.

"I know not," answered the Saint; "what seems it to be, brother?"

"I have been watching it," said the other, "and I think it grows. Look! it is even now higher than when first you looked; is it not so?"

And sure enough, Gudwall saw that ever so little at a time the brown patch was growing and spreading from right to left. Grain by grain the sand bar rose higher and higher till it thrust bravely above the blueness a solid wall extending for some distance through the water in front of the cave. Against this new breakwater the surf roared and foamed in terrible rage, but it could not pass, it could no longer swoop down into the cavern as it had done before.

"The Lord has given us a defense," said Gudwall with a thankful heart. And then his eye caught sight of a great bluefish swimming back into the deep sea. "It is the fish who have built us the wall," he cried. "Blessed be the fish who have this day helped us in our need."

For the fish had piled up a stout and lasting barrier between Saint Gudwall and the angry sea, and thenceforth he could live in his cave safely during both summer and winter.

The Ballad of Saint Giles and the Deer

All in the forest far away
    Where no one ever came,
There dwelt a good man, old and gray,—
    Saint Giles the hermit's name.

His forest home a rocky cave
    Beneath an aspen tree;
And for his friend Saint Giles did have
    A Deer, who wandered free.

A gentle red and mottled Deer
    Who made her home close by,
Who at his call came without fear,
    Forgetting to be shy.

Sure never all in lovely France
    Was there a Deer so tame;
Ah, but to see her start and prance
    When he would call her name!

She gave him milk, his simple fare,
    And browsed upon the green,
Ah, such a gentle, loving pair
    I wis was never seen.

And he was happy in his cell,
    And joyous 'neath his trees,
Content with woodland beasts to dwell,
    His only neighbors these.

Saints and Friendly Beasts

The wood was dark, the wood was grim,
    And never till one day
Had human voices troubled him,
    Or world-folk passed that way.

But on a dewy springtime morn
    When April climbed the hill,
There came the wind of silver horn,
    Halloos and whistles shrill;

The galloping of horses' feet,
    The bloody bay of hounds,
Broke through the forest silence sweet
    And echoed deadly sounds.

Saint Giles sat in his lonely cell,
    Whenas the rout drew nigh;
But at the noise his kind heart fell
    And sorrow dimmed his eye.

He loved not men who hunt to kill,
    Loved not the rich and grand,
For in those days the Pagans still
    Held lordship in the land.

But scarcely had he reached the door
    And seized his staff of oak,
When like a billow with a roar
    The chase upon him broke.

With one last hope of dear escape,
    Into the open space
Bounded a light and graceful shape,
    The quarry of the chase.

The Ballad of Saint Giles and the Deer

All flecked with foam, all quivering
    With weariness and fear,
Crouched at his feet the hunted thing,
    His gentle friend, the Deer.

Behind her bayed the pack of hounds,
    Their cruel teeth gleamed white,
Nearing with eager leaps and bounds;
    He turned sick at the sight.

Saint Giles looked down upon the Deer,
    Saint Giles looked up again,
He saw the danger drawing near,
    The death, with all its pain.

He laid his hand upon her head,
    The soft head of his friend, —
"And shall I let thee die?" he said,
    "And watch thy hapless end?"

He stooped and gently murmured, "Nay!"
    Stroking her mottled side,
He stepped before her where she lay;
    "They slay me first!" he cried.

Her frightened eyes looked up at him,
    Her little heart beat high,
She trembled sore in every limb, —
    The bushes parted nigh.

"Halloo! Halloo!" the huntsmen cried
    As through the hedge they burst;
An archer all in green espied
    The crouching quarry first.

Swift as a thought his arrow flew,
    Saint Giles threw out his arm,
Alack! the aim was all too true,
    Saint Giles must bear the harm.

The arrow pierced too well, too well;
    All in that mournful wood
Saint Giles upon the greensward fell,
    And dyed it with his blood.

He fell, but falling laid his hand
    Upon the trembling Deer, —
"My life for hers, dost understand?"
    He cried so all could hear.

Now as upon the green he lay
    All in a deathly swound,
The King dashed up with courtiers gay
    And looked upon his wound.

The King rode up, and "Ho!" he cried,
    "Whom find we in our wood?
Who spares the deer with mottled hide?
    Who sheds an old man's blood?"

The King looked down with ruthful eye
    When all the thing was told,
"Alack!" he cried, "he must not die,
    So kind a man and bold.

"Bear me the Saint into his cave;
    Who falls to save his friend
Deserves for leech his King to have;
    I will his pallet tend."

The Ballad of Saint Giles and the Deer

They spared to him the sore-bought Deer;
    And in that lowly cell
For many weary days and drear
    The King came there to dwell.

The King, who was a godless man,
    A pagan, heart and soul,
Played nurse until the wound began
    To heal, and Giles was whole.

But in the little forest cave
    The King learned many things
Known to the meanest Christian slave,
    But secrets from the kings.

For good Saint Giles had won his heart
    By his brave deed and bold,
And ere the great King did depart
    His Christian faith he told.

And while the red Deer stood beside,
    The King gave Giles his word
That e'er a Christian he would bide,
    And keep what he had heard.

And so the monarch rode away
    And left the two alone,
Saint Giles a happy man that day,
    The good Deer still his own.

Safe from the eager hunting horde
    The Saint would keep his friend,
Protected by the King's own word
    Thenceforth unto the end.

For unmolested in his cell,
    Careless of everything
Giles with his friendly Deer could dwell
    Liege to a Christian King.

The Wolf-Mother of Saint Ailbe

This is the story of a poor little Irish baby whose cruel father and mother did not care anything about him. But because they could not sell him nor give him away they tried to lose him. They wrapped him in a piece of cloth and took him up on the mountain side, and there they left him lying all alone on a bush of heather.

Now an old mother wolf was out taking her evening walk on the mountain after tending her babies in the den all day. And just as she was passing the heather bush she heard a faint, funny little cry. She pricked up her pointed ears and said, "What's that!" And lo and behold, when she came to sniff out the mystery with her keen nose, it led her straight to the spot where the little pink baby lay, crying with cold and hunger.

The heart of the kind mother wolf was touched, for she thought of her own little ones at home, and how sad it would be to see them so helpless and lonely and forgotten. So she picked the baby up in her mouth carefully and ran home with him to her den in the rocks at the foot of the mountain. Here the little one, whose name was Ailbe, lived with the baby wolves, sharing their breakfast and dinner and supper, playing and quarreling and growing up with them. The wolf-mother took good care of him and saw that he had the best of everything, for she loved him dearly indeed. And Ailbe grew stronger and stronger, taller and taller, handsomer and handsomer every day, living his happy life in the wild woods of green Ireland.

Now one day, a year or two after this, a hunter came riding over the mountain on his way home from the chase, and he happened to pass near the cave where Ailbe and the wolves lived. As he was riding along under the trees he saw a little white creature run across the path in front of him. At first he thought it was a rabbit; but it was too big for a rabbit, and besides it did not hop. The hunter jumped down from his horse and ran after the funny animal to find out what it was. His long legs soon overtook it in a clump of bushes where it was hiding, and imagine the hunter's surprise when he found that it had neither fur nor horns nor four feet nor a tail, but that it was a beautiful child who could not stand upright, and whose little bare body ran on all-fours like a baby wolf! It was little Ailbe, the wolf-mother's pet, who had grown so fast that he was almost able to take care of himself. But he was not quite able, the hunter thought; and he said to himself that he would carry the poor little thing home to his kind wife, that she might take care of him. So he caught Ailbe up in his arms, kicking and squealing and biting like the wild little animal he was, and wrapped him in a corner of his great cloak. Then he jumped on his horse with a chirrup and galloped away out of the woods towards his village.

But Ailbe did not want to leave his forest home, the wolf-den, and his little wolf brothers. Especially he did not want to leave his dear foster mother. So he screamed and struggled to get away from the big hunter, and he called to the wolves in their own language to come and help him. Then out of the forest came bounding the great mother wolf with her four children, now grown to be nearly as big as herself. She chased after the fleeting horse and snapped at the loose end of the huntsman's cloak, howling with grief and anger. But she could not catch the thief, nor get back her adopted son, the little smooth-skinned foundling. So after following them for miles, the five wolves gradually dropped further and further behind. And at last, as he stretched out his little arms to them over the hunter's velvet shoulder, Ailbe saw them stop in the road panting, with one last howl of farewell. They had given up the hopeless chase. And with their tails between their legs and their heads drooping low they slunk back to their lonely den where they would never see their little boy playmate any more. It was a sad day for good wolf-mother.

But the hunter carried little Ailbe home with him on the horse's back. And he found a new mother there to receive him. Ailbe never knew who his first mother was, but she must have been a bad, cruel woman. His second mother was the kind wolf. And this one, the third, was a beautiful Princess.

For the hunter who had found the child was a Prince, and he lived in a grand castle by a lake near Tipperary, with hundreds of servants and horses and dogs and little pages for Ailbe to play with. And here he lived and was very happy; and here he learned all the things which in those days made a little boy grow up into a wise and great

The Wolf-Mother of Saint Ailbe

man. He grew up so wise and great that he was made a Bishop and had a palace of his own in the town of Emly. People came to see him from far and near, who made him presents, and asked him questions, and ate his dinners.

But though he had grown so great and famous Ailbe had never forgotten his second mother, the good wolf, nor his four-footed brothers, in their coats of gray fur. And sometimes when his visitors were stupid and stayed a long time, or when they asked too many questions, or when they made him presents which he did not like, Ailbe longed to be back in the forest with the good beasts. For they had much more sense, though they had never kissed the Blarney Stone, which makes one talk good Irish.

A great many years afterwards there was one day a huge hunt in Emly. All the lords for miles around were out chasing the wild beasts, and among them was the Prince, Ailbe's foster-father. But the Bishop himself was not with them. He did not see any sport in killing poor creatures. It was almost night, and the people of Emly were out watching for the hunters to return. The Bishop was coming down the village street on his way from church, when the sound of horns came over the hills close by, and he knew the chase was nearing home.

Louder and louder came the "tantara-tara!" of the horns, and then he could hear the gallopy thud of the horses' hoofs and the yelp of the hounds. But suddenly the Bishop's heart stood still. Among all the other noises of the chase he heard a sound which made him think — think — think. It was the long-drawn howl of a wolf, a sad howl of fear and weariness and pain. It spoke a language which he had almost forgotten. But hardly had he time to think again and to remember, before down the village street came a great gaunt figure, flying in long leaps from the foremost dogs who were snapping at her heels. It was Ailbe's wolf-mother.

He recognized her as soon as he saw her green eyes and the patch of white on her light foreleg. And she recognized him, too, — how I cannot say, for he had changed greatly since she last saw him, a naked little sunbrowned boy. But at any rate, in his fine robes of purple and linen and rich lace, with the mitre on his head and the crozier in his hand, the wolf-mother knew her dear son. With a cry of joy she bounded up to him and laid her head on his breast, as if she knew he would protect her from the growling dogs and the fierce-eyed hunters. And the good Bishop was true to her. For he drew his beautiful velvet cloak about her tired, panting body, and laid his hand lovingly on her head. Then in the other he held up his crook warningly to keep back the ferocious dogs.

"I will protect thee, old mother," he said tenderly. "When I was little and young and feeble, thou didst nourish and cherish and protect me; and now that thou art old and gray and weak, shall I not render the same love and care to thee? None shall injure thee."

Then the hunters came tearing up on their foaming horses and stopped short to find what the matter was. Some of them were angry and wanted even now to kill the poor wolf, just as the dogs did who were prowling about snarling with disappointment. But Ailbe would have none of it. He forbade them to touch the wolf. And he was so powerful and wise and holy that they dared not disobey him, but had to be content with seeing their hunt spoiled and their prey taken out of their clutches.

But before the hunters and their dogs rode away, Saint Ailbe had something more to say to them. And he bade all the curious townsfolk who had gathered about him and the wolf to listen also. He repeated the promise which he had made to the wolf, and warned every one thenceforth not to hurt her or her children, either in the village, or in the woods, or on the mountain. And turning to her once more he said: —

"See, mother, you need not fear. They dare not hurt you now you have found your son to protect you. Come every day with my brothers to my table, and you and yours shall share my food, as once I so often shared yours."

And so it was. Every day after that so long as she lived the old wolf-mother brought her four children to the Bishop's palace and howled at the gate for the porter to let them in. And every day he opened to them, and the steward showed the five into the great dining hall where Ailbe sat at the head of the table, with five places set for the rest of the family. And there with her five dear children about her in a happy circle the kind wolf-mother sat and ate the good things which the Bishop's friends had sent him. But the child she loved best was none of those in furry coats and fine whiskers who looked like her; it was the blue-eyed Saint at the top of the table in his robes of purple and white.

But Saint Ailbe would look about him at his mother and his brothers and would laugh contentedly.

"What a handsome family we are!" he would say. And it was true.

Saint Rigobert's Dinner

Saint Rigobert was hungry. He had eaten nothing that morning, neither had little Pierre, his serving lad, who trotted along before him on the road to Rheims. They were going to visit Wibert, the Deputy-Governor of Rheims, to pay him some money which the Bishop owed, — all the money which he had in the world. And that is why they had nothing left to buy them a breakfast, and why little Pierre gazed into the bakers' shops so hungrily and licked his lips as they passed. Good Saint Rigobert did not see the windows of buns and tarts and pasties as they went along, for his eyes were bent upon the ground and he was singing hymns over to himself under his breath. Still, he too was very faint.

Saint Rigobert was poor. He was a good old Bishop; but the King of France did not love him, and had sent him away from the court and the big, rich city to live among the poor folk in the country. Saint Rigobert did not mind this very much, for he loved the pretty little village of Gernicour where he lived. He loved the people who dwelled there, too; and especially he loved Pierre, who had come to his home to be his little page and helper.

The people of the village meant to be kind and generous; but they were mostly stupid folk who saw only what was in front of their noses. And they did not guess how very poor their dear Bishop was. They were poor, too, and had to be careful of their little bits of money. But they all had vegetables and milk and eggs and butter, and if every one had helped a little, as they ought, — for he was always doing kind things for them, — Saint Rigobert would not have gone hungry so often.

It made the Bishop sorry to find them so careless, but he never complained. He would not tell them, nor beg them to help him, and often even little Pierre did not know how long he fasted. For he would give the boy all the supper and keep none himself. But he was always cheery and contented. He always had a kind word for the people as he passed them on the street. And when he went to the big town of Rheims near by he never complained to the Governor there about what a poor, miserable parish he lived in, or how little the people of Gernicour did for their Bishop. For he liked to believe that they did the best they could.

And that is why, when the two came into Wibert's hall, Saint Rigobert paid the money to the Governor without a word of his hunger or his faintness. And even when he saw the great table laid for dinner and the smoking dishes brought in by a procession of serving men, he turned away resolutely and tried not to show how tempting the good things looked and smelled. He gathered up the folds of his robe, and taking his Bishop's staff in his hand, rose to go back to Gernicour and his dinnerless house. But as they were leaving the hall, Pierre trailing out very reluctantly with many a backward look, Wibert the governor called them back. Perhaps he had seen the longing in the eyes of little Pierre as the great haunch of venison was set on the board. Perhaps he had noticed how pale and hollow Saint Rigobert's cheeks were, and half guessed the cause. At all events he said kindly: —

"I pray thee, stay and dine with us, thou and the boy yonder. See, the meat is ready, and there is room for many more at table."

But Saint Rigobert had a service to hold in the church at Gernicour, and knew they had barely time to reach home if they walked briskly. Besides, he was too proud to accept charity, and for the sake of his people he feared to let the Governor see how very hungry he was.

"Nay," he answered gently, "I thank thee for thy courtesy, friend Wibert. But we may not tarry. The time scants us for a dinner before the service in the church at Gernicour, and we must hasten or we be late. Come, lad, we must be stirring anon."

Tears of disappointment were standing in Pierre's eyes, he wanted so much to stay and have some of that good dinner. But he never thought of questioning his master's commands. The Governor pressed them to stay, but Rigobert was firm, and passed on to the door, Pierre following sulkily behind. But just as they reached the door there was a commotion outside, and the sound of quacking and men's laughter. And there came in a serving man bearing in his arms a great white goose, which was flapping his wings and cackling hoarsely in fright.

"Ho, what have we here?" said the Governor crossly. "Why do you

Saint Rigobert's Dinner

let such a commotion into my hall, you fellow?"

"Please you, sir," answered the serving man as well as he could with the goose struggling in his arms, "this goose is a tribute from the widow Rene, and she begs your Honor to accept him as a poor present."

"A poor present indeed," said the Governor testily. "What do I want of the creature? We have more fowls now than we know what to do with. I wish him not." Then an idea came into his head, and he turned to Saint Rigobert. "Why, reverend sir," he said laughing, "since you will not stay to dine with me, I prithee take this fat fellow home with you, for dinner in Gernicour. 'Twill be a good riddance for us, in sooth."

Saint Rigobert hesitated. But seeing the look of eagerness in Pierre's face he concluded to accept the gift, which was a common one enough in those days.

"Grammercy for your courtesy, Master Wibert," he answered. "We take your bounty of the fine goose, since it seemeth that your tables have space for little more. Now then, Pierre lad, take up thy prey. And look he bite thee not," he added as the boy made haste to seize the great struggling bird.

The goose pecked and squawked and flapped horribly while Pierre was getting his arms about him. But finally they were ready to start, Pierre going first with the goose who was nearly as big as himself, and the Bishop following grasping his staff, his eyes bent upon the ground.

Pierre's heart was full of joy. He chuckled and laughed and could hardly wait till they should reach home, for thinking of the fine dinner at the end of the road. But Saint Rigobert had already forgotten the goose; he had so many other things to think about. That is the way he had taught himself to forget how hungry he was — he just thought about something else. But all on a sudden Rigobert was startled by a great cackle and a scream in front of him down the road. He looked up just in time to see a big white thing sailing away into the sky, and Pierre hopping up and down in the road screaming and crying.

The Bishop overtook the little fellow quickly. "Lad, lad, hast thou lost thy goose?" he asked gently.

"Oh Father," sobbed the boy, "our nice dinner! Your dinner, master! The wicked goose has flown away. Oh, what a careless boy I am to let him 'scape me so!" And he sat down on a stone and cried as if his heart would break.

"Nay, nay," the good Bishop said, patting him on the head soothingly, "perhaps the poor goose did not want to be roasted, Pierre. Can you blame him for seeking his liberty instead? I find no fault with him; but I am sorry for thy dinner, lad. We must try to get something else. Cheer up, Pierre, let the white goose go. All will yet be well, lad."

He made Pierre get up, still crying bitterly, and on they trudged again along the dusty road. But this time there was no dinner for them to look forward to, and the way seemed very long. Pierre dragged his feet heavily, and it seemed as if he could not go another step with that emptiness in his stomach and the ache in his head. But again Saint Rigobert began to hum his hymns softly under his breath, keeping time to the beat of his aged feet on the dusty road. The loss of his dinner seemed to trouble him little. Perhaps he was secretly glad that the poor goose had escaped; for he was very tenderhearted and loved not to have creatures killed, even for food.

They had gone quite a little distance, and Rigobert began to sing louder and louder as they neared his church. When suddenly there came a strange sound in the air over his head. And then with a great fluttering a big white goose came circling down right before Saint Rigobert's feet. The good Saint stopped short in surprise, and Pierre, turning about, could hardly believe his eyes. But sure enough, there was the very same goose, looking up into Saint Rigobert's face and cackling as if trying to tell him something.

"I didn't mean to run away," he seemed to say. "I didn't know you were hungry, holy man, and that I was taking away your dinner. Sing on and I will follow you home."

Pierre turned and ran back to the goose and would have seized him by the neck so he could not get away again. But Saint Rigobert held up his finger warningly, and the boy stood still.

"Do not touch him, Pierre," said the Bishop earnestly. "I do not think he will run away. Let us see."

And sure enough, when they started on once more, Saint Rigobert still singing softly, Pierre, who kept glancing back, saw the goose waddling slowly at his master's heels. So the queer little procession came into Gernicour; and every one stopped along the streets with open mouths, wondering to see them pass. At last they reached the Bishop's house. And there Rigobert ceased his singing, and turning to the goose stroked his feathers gently and said: —

"Good friend, thou hast been faithful. Thou shalt be rewarded. Aye, ruffle up thy feathers, good goose, for they shall never be plucked from thee, nor shalt thou be cooked for food. Thou art my friend from to-day. No pen shall hold thee, but thou shalt follow me as thou wilt."

And the Saint kept his promise. For after that the goose lived with him in happiness and peace. They would take long walks together in the fields about Gernicour. They made visits to the sick and the sorrowful. Indeed, wherever Saint Rigobert went the goose followed close at his heels like a dog. Even when Rigobert went again to see the Governor of Rheims, the goose waddled all the way there and back along the crooked road over part of which he had gone that first time in little Pierre's arms. And how the Governor did laugh as he stood in his door and watched the strange pair disappear down the road.

"He could not have been very hungry after all," the Governor thought, "or I should never have seen that goose again." Which shows how little even a Governor knows about some things.

More than this, whenever Rigobert went to hold service in his little church the goose escorted him there also. But he knew better than to go inside. He would wait by the porch, preening his feathers in the sunshine and snapping bugs in the grass of the churchyard until his dear master came out. And then he would escort him back home again. He was a very well-mannered goose.

But dear me! All this time I have left poor little Pierre standing with a quivering chin outside the Bishop's door, hopeless of a dinner. But it all came right, just as the Bishop had said it would. I must tell you about that. For when Rigobert returned from church that same day feeling very faint and hungry indeed, after the long walk and the excitement of the goose-hap, Pierre came running out to meet him with a smiling face.

"Oh Father, Father!" he cried. "We are to have a dinner, after all.

Come quick, I am so hungry I cannot wait! The village folk have heard about the pious goose who came back to be your dinner, and how you would not eat him. And so they have sent us a basket of good things instead. And they promise that never again so long as they have anything to eat themselves shall we be hungry any more. Oh Father! I am so glad we did not eat the goose."

And good Saint Rigobert laid his hand on Pierre's head and said, "Dear lad, you will never be sorry for showing kindness to a friendly bird or beast." Then the goose came quacking up to them and they all three went into the house together to eat their good, good dinner.

Saint Francis of Assisi

Barefooted in the snow, bareheaded in the rain, Saint Francis wandered up and down the world smiling for the great love that was in his heart.

And because it grew from love the smile of Saint Francis was a wonderful thing. It opened the hearts of men and coaxed the secrets of their thoughts. It led human folk whithersoever Saint Francis willed. It drew the beasts to his side and the birds to nestle in his bosom. It was like a magic charm.

Great princes knew his smile and they obeyed its command to be generous and good. The sick and sorrowful knew his smile. It meant healing and comfort. Then they rose and blessed God in the name of Saint Francis. The wretched beggars in the streets of Assisi knew it. To them the smile of "the Lord's own beggar" meant help and sympathy. Like them he was poor and homeless, often ill and hungry. They wondered that he could smile. But he said,

"It does not become a servant of God to have an air of melancholy and a face full of trouble." So they also tried to smile, poor fellows. But how different it was!

The little lambs to whom he gave his special protection and care knew the smile of Saint Francis. Once he met two woolly lambkins who were being carried to market. He never had any money, but taking off his cloak, which was all he had to part with, he gave it to buy their lives. And he carried the lambs home in his bosom.

The wilder beasts beyond the mountains, the fierce wolves and shy foxes of Syria and Spain whom he met in his wanderings knew Saint Francis. Here was a brother who was not afraid of them and whom they could trust in return, a brother who understood and sympathized. The birds in the trees knew also, and his coming was the signal of peace. Then they sang with Francis, but he was the sweetest singer of them all.

Besides these living things the green fields of Italy, the trees, the meadows, the brooks, the flowers all knew the smile of Saint Francis. It meant to them many things which only a poet can tell. But Francis understood, for he was a poet.

Upon all alike his face of love beamed tenderly. For Saint Francis of Assisi was a little brother of the whole great world and of all created things. Not only did his heart warm to Brother Sheep and Sister Bees, to his Brother Fish and his little Sisters the Doves, but he called the Sun and Wind his brothers and the Moon and Water his sisters. Of all the saints about whom the legends tell, Francis was the gentlest and most loving. And if

> "He prayeth best who loveth best
> All things both great and small,"

the prayers of Saint Francis must have been very dear to Him who "made and loveth all."

There was none so poor as Francis. Not a penny did he have, not a penny would he touch. Let them be given to those who could not smile, he said. His food he begged from door to door, broken crusts for a single poor meal; more he would not take. His sleeping place was the floor or the haymow, the ruined church, whatever lodging chance gave him. Oftenest he slept upon the bare ground with a stone for his pillow. He wanted to be poor because Christ was poor, and he was trying to live like his Master.

In his coarse brown gown, tied about the waist with a rope, without hat or shoes he wandered singing, smiling. The love which beamed from him like radiance from a star shone back from every pair of eyes which looked into his own. For all the world loved Francis in the time of the Crusades. And even to-day, seven hundred years since that dear beggar passed cheerily up and down the rough Italian roads, — even to-day there are many who love him like a lost elder brother.

Saint Francis preached to all lessons of charity and peace. His were simple words, for he had not the wisdom of many books. But he knew the book of the human heart from cover to cover. His words were like fire, they warmed and wakened. No one could resist the entreaty and the love that was in them. So thousands joined the Society of Little Brothers of which he was the founder, and became his helpers in works of charity and holiness.

SAINT FRANCIS OF ASSISI

His church was out of doors in the beautiful world that he loved, in mountain, field, or forest, wherever he happened to be wandering. Sometimes he preached by the candle-light of stars. Often the cloistering trees along the roadside made his chapel, and the blue sky was the only roof between him and heaven. Often his choir was of the brother birds in the branches and his congregation a group of brother beasts. For he preached to them also who, though they spoke a different language, were yet children of his Father. And in his little talks to them he always showed the courtesy which one brother owes another.

Once, on returning from a journey beyond the sea, he was traveling through the Venetian country, when he heard a great congregation of birds singing among the bushes. And he said to his companion, "Our sisters, the birds, are praising their Maker. Let us then go into their midst and sing." So they did this, and the birds did not fly away but continued to sing so loudly that the brothers could not hear each other. Then Saint Francis turned to the birds and said politely, "Sisters, cease your song until we have rendered our bounden praise to God!" So the birds were still until the brothers had finished their psalm. But after that when it was again their turn the birds went on with their song.

At another time when he was preaching in the town of Alvia among the hills, the swallows flew about and twittered so loudly that the people could not hear Saint Francis' voice. The birds did not mean to be rude, however. So he turned to the swallows and saluted them courteously. "My sisters," he said, "it is now time that I should speak. Since you have had your say, listen now in your turn to the word of God and be silent till the sermon is finished." And again the birds obeyed the smile and the voice of him who loved them. Though whether they understood the grown-up sermon that followed I cannot tell.

But this is the little sermon which he made one day for a congregation of birds who sat around him in the bushes listening.

"Brother Birds, greatly are ye bound to praise the Creator who clotheth you with feathers and giveth you wings to fly with and a purer air to breathe; and who careth for you who have so little care for yourselves."

It was not a long sermon, so the birds could not have grown tired or sleepy, and I am sure they understood every word. So after he had given them his blessing he let them go, and they went singing as he had bidden them.

Saint Francis preached the lessons of peace; he would not have cruelty or bloodshed among his human friends. And he also taught his beasts to be kind. He loved best the gentle lambs, one of which was almost always with him, and in his sermons he would point to them to show men what their lives should be. But there is a story told of the lesson he taught a wolf that shows what power the Saint had over the fiercer animals. There are many stories of wolves whom the saints made tame. But this wolf of Saint Francis was the most terrible of them all.

This huge and savage wolf had been causing great horror to the people of Gubbio. For in the night he not only stole sheep and cows from the farms, but he came and carried off men also for his dinner. So that people were afraid to go out of the town for fear of being gobbled up.

Now Saint Francis came. And he said, "I will go out and seek this wolf." But the townsfolk begged him not to go, for the good man was dear to them and they feared never to see him again. However, he was resolved and went forth from the gate.

He had gone but a little way when out rushed the wolf to meet him, with his mouth wide open, roaring horribly. Then Saint Francis made the sign of the cross and said gently: —

"Come hither, Brother Wolf. I command thee in Christ's behalf that thou do no evil to me nor to any one." And wonderful to say! The wolf grew tame and came like a lamb to lie at Saint Francis' feet.

Then Francis went on to rebuke him, saying that he deserved to be hung for his many sins, being a robber and a wicked murderer of men and beasts.

"But I wish, Brother Wolf," he said, "to make peace between thee and men; therefore vex them no more and they will pardon thee all thy past offenses, and neither dogs nor men will chase thee any more."

At this the wolf wagged his tail and bowed his head to show he understood. And putting his right paw in the hand of Saint Francis he promised never again to steal nor slay. Then like a gentle dog he followed the holy man to the market-place of the town, where great crowds of people had gathered to see what Saint Francis would do with the great beast, their enemy, for they thought he was to be punished. But Francis rose and said to them: —

"Hearken, dear brethren: Brother Wolf who is here before you has promised me that he will make peace with you and will never injure you in any way, if ye promise to give him day by day what is needful for his dinner. And I will be surety for him." Thereupon with a great shout all the people promised to give him his daily food. Again the wolf wagged his tail, flapped his long ears, bowed his head, and gave his paw to Saint Francis to show that he would keep his word. All the people saw him do this. And then there were shouts of wonder you may be sure, and great rejoicing because Saint Francis had saved them from this cruel beast, and had made a gentle friend of their dreaded enemy.

So after this the wolf lived two years at Gubbio and went about from door to door humbly begging his food like Saint Francis himself. He never harmed any one, not even the little children who teased and pulled him about. But all the people loved him and gave him what he liked to eat; and not even a dog would bark at his heels or growl at the friend of Saint Francis. So he lived to a good old age. And when after two years Brother Wolf died because he was so old, the citizens were very sorrowful. For not only did they miss the soft pat-pat of his steps passing through the city, but they grieved for the sorrow of Saint Francis in losing a kindly friend, — Saint Francis of whose saintliness and power the humble beast had been a daily reminder.

Francis could not bear to see a little brother in trouble or pain, and this the beasts knew very well. He would not willingly tread upon an insect, but would step aside and gently bid the Brother Worm depart in peace. The fish which a fisherman gave him he restored to the water, where it played about his boat and would not leave him till he bade it go.

Once again in the village of Gubbio a live baby hare was brought him as a present, for his breakfast. But when Francis saw the frightened look of the little creature held in the arms of one of the brothers, his heart ached with sympathy.

"Little Brother Leveret, come to me," he said. "Why hast thou let thyself be taken?" And the little fellow as if understanding the invitation jumped out of the friar's arms and ran to Francis, hiding in the

Saint Francis of Assisi

folds of his gown. But when Francis took it out and set it free, very politely giving it permission to depart instead of staying to make a breakfast, it would not go. Again and again it returned nestling to its new-found friend, as if guessing that here at least it would be safe forever. But at last tenderly Saint Francis sent the good brother away with it into the wood, where it was safe once more among its little bob-tailed brothers and sisters.

Now after a life spent like Christ's in works of poverty, charity, and love, Saint Francis came at last to have one spot in the world which he could call his own. It was neither a church nor a convent, a cottage nor even a cell. It was only a bare and lonely mountain top where wild beasts lived and wild birds had a home. This retreat in the wilderness was the gift which Orlando, a rich nobleman, chose to make Saint Francis. And it was a precious gift indeed, sorely needed by the Lord's weary beggar. For he was worn with wandering; he was ill and weak, and his gentle eyes were growing dim so that he could not go along the winding ways. But he was happy still.

So one warm September day he went with some of his chosen brethren to take possession of their new home. They left the villages, the farms, and at last even the scattered shepherds' huts far below and behind them, and came into the quiet of the Italian hills.

They climbed and climbed over the rocks and along the ravines, till they came in sight of the bald summit where Francis was to dwell. And here in happy weariness he paused to rest under an oak-tree and look about upon the beautiful scene.

But suddenly the air was filled with music, a chorus of trills and quavers and carols of the wildest joy. Then the air grew dark with whirring wings. The birds of the mountain were coming from everywhere to welcome home their brother. They flew to him by hundreds, perching on his head and shoulders; and when every other spot was covered they twittered into the hood of his brown mantle. The brothers stood about, wondering greatly, although they had seen Saint Francis in some such plight before. But the peasant who led the ass which had brought Saint Francis so far stood like one turned to stone, unable to believe his eyes. Here was a miracle the like of which he had never dreamed.

But Saint Francis was filled with gladness. "Dearest brethren," he said, "I think it must be pleasant to our Lord that we should dwell in this solitary place, since our brothers and sisters the birds are so glad of our coming."

And indeed, how could they help being glad of his coming, the dear, kind Saint?

And how they hovered around the shelter of branches which the brethren built for him under a beech-tree on the very mountain top! One can picture them at morning, noon, and night joining in his songs of praise, or keeping polite silence while the holy man talked with God.

Many wonderful things happened upon the Monte Alverno while Saint Francis dwelt there. But none were more wonderful than the great love of Francis himself; his love which was so big and so wide that it wrapped the whole round world, binding all creatures more closely in a common brotherhood.

So that every man and every bird and every beast that lives ought to love the name of that dear Saint, their childlike, simple, happy little brother, Saint Francis of Assisi.

HERE
THE BOOK OF
SAINTS & FRIENDLY BEASTS
ENDS

Editor's Note: If you enjoyed this collection, be sure to get *Legends of the Norse Gods: In the Days of Giants* by Abbie Farwell Brown, published for the Folklore and Mythology Archive by Kalevala Books.

Calendar

Here Follow the Days
of the Saints and Their Beasts

Jan. 4.	Saint Rigobert.
Jan. 13.	Saint Kentigern.
Jan. 14.	Saint Felix.
Jan. 18.	Saint Prisca.
Jan. 19.	Saint Launomar.
Feb. 1.	Saint Bridget.
Feb. 3.	Saint Werburgh.
	Saint Blaise.
Feb. 9.	Saint Athracta.
Feb. 14.	Saint Berach.
March 5.	Saint Gerasimus.
March 20.	Saint Cuthbert.
April 14.	Saint Fronto.
May 10.	Saint Comgall.
June 6.	Saint Gudwall.
June 18.	Saint Hervé.
August 1.	Saint Keneth.
Sept. 1.	Saint Giles.
Sept. 12.	Saint Ailbe.
Oct. 4.	Saint Francis.

Also Published by Kalevala Books

Swedish Fairy Tales:
Legends of Trolls, Elves, Fairies, and Giants
by Herman Hofberg; translated by W. H. Myers

Travel back to a magical world of colorful myth and legend as you explore this collection of folktales from Sweden. Over eighty stories are told, with more than forty illustrations of trolls, ghosts, giants, and other denizens of the Swedish folkscape. There are tales of lost treasure, encounters with the devil, meetings with the *tomte*, the spirits of the home, and of the beautiful wood nymphs, whose true nature is often betrayed by a fox tail peeking below the hem of a skirt. *Swedish Fairy Tales,* originally published in 1890, will dazzle a new generation of readers with legends from Sweden's early story-telling tradition.

ISBN-13: 978-1880954096

The Piper Came to Our Town:
Bagpipe Folklore, Legends, and Fairy Tales
by Joanne Asala

The bagpipes have a long and noble history stretching back centuries. They have been played across Scotland, Ireland, Continental Europe, and the Middle East, and are found in such diverse places as India and the Americas. *The Piper Came to Our Town* is a collection of over seventy stories, tales, anecdotes, and legends of pipers, running the gamut from the ordinary to the supernatural. You will travel from the battlefields of Africa to faerie caves below the earth, and meet pipers urging troops to victory, fighting off man-eating cows, and even creating new worlds. *The Piper Came to Our Town* will delight fans of bagpipe music, lore, and tradition, as well as anyone who likes a good folk story.

ISBN-13: 978-1880954034

Turf Fire Stories and Fairy Tales of Ireland: A Collection of Irish Myth and Legend
by Barry O'Connor

Turf Fire Stories and Fairy Tales of Ireland is a delightful collection of tales not found anywhere else. Stories include "The Four Leaved Shamrock," "Blarney Castle," "Murder Will Out," "Smuggled Poteen," "The Irish Whistle," "The Fairy's Purse," "The Magic Clover," "The Wishing Stone," and many more. With fifty-six tales in all, there's something to please every fan of Irish myth and legend.

ISBN-13: 978-1880954119

Tales and Legends of Sweden and Norway
by M. G. Sleeper

Tales and Legends of Sweden and Norway is not your average folktale collection. Originally published in 1867 as part of the Fonthill Recreation series, it is full of descriptions of characters, customs, costumes, and occupations of the Scandinavian people, along with a great deal of myth, songs, legends, and history. The storytelling takes the form of a conversation between a well-travelled uncle, who lives at Fonthill, and his nephews and nieces. These conversations and stories are written down from the perspective of the eldest child, a school-girl of sixteen, who intersperses them with descriptions of the family recreations, the walks, the drives, visits, guests, and plays, and also with the spicy stories told at various periods for the entertainment of the home-circle, either by its own members, or by the visitors at the house. Look for other titles in the Fonthill series, including *Tales and Legends of the Mediterranean Islands*, soon to be published as part of the Folklore and Mythology Archive.

ISBN-13: 978-1-880954126

Also Published by Kalevala Books

**Myths and Folk Tales of Celtic France:
Legends and Romances of Brittany**
by Lewis Spence

Brittany (Breizh) occupies a large peninsula in the northwest corner of France, lying between the English Channel to the north and the Bay of Biscay to the south. It is one of the six Celtic Nations, the others being Cornwall (Kernow), Ireland (Éire), Isle of Man (Mannin), Scotland (Alba), and Wales (Cymru). In each of these regions the Celtic languages and cultural traits have survived to this day. In 1917, noted folklorist Lewis Spence first published this amazing collection of fairy tales and legends of the Breton people. Chapters include: "The Land, The People, and Their Story;" "Menhirs and Dolmens;" "The Fairies of Brittany;" "Sprites and Demons of Brittany;" "World Tales in Brittany;" "Breton Folk Tales;" "Popular Legends of Brittany;" "Hero-Tales of Brittany;" "The Black Art and Its Ministers;" "Arthurian Romance in Brittany;" "The Breton Lays of Marie de France;" "The Saints of Brittany;" and "Costumes and Customs of Brittany." *Myths and Folk Tales of Celtic France* is a welcome addition to any collection of Celtic myth, magic, and tradition.

ISBN: 978-1-880954133

**A Book of Giants
Tales of Very Tall Men of Myth, Legend, History, and Science**
by Henry Wysham Lanier

Many mythologies, folk tales, and legends of the world include stories of giants, monsters who may resemble human, but who are of great size and even greater strength. In the earliest tales, giants often predate the gods themselves, struggling against them for dominion of the earth. In 1922, author and editor Henry Wysham Lanier collected tales of giants from all over the globe. This entertaining anthology features both the familiar and unfamiliar and is sure to please any fan of myth and folklore.

ISBN: 978-1-880954140

Hero Tales and Legends of the Rhine: Folklore and Myths from Switzerland, Liechtenstein, Austria, Germany, France, and the Netherlands
by Lewis Spence

Along with the Danube River, the Rhine once served as the northern frontier of the Roman Empire. Romans considered the Rhine as the outermost border of civilization; beyond its waters dwelt strange, mythical creatures and wild pagan tribes. The legends that arose in this region are filled with stories of dragons, water nymphs, and brave warrior heroes. In 1915, folklorist Lewis Spence gathered and published many of these stories as *Hero Tales and Legends of the Rhine*, including: "The Battle of Skeletons;" "The Lorelei;" "The Forsaken Bride;" "The Nixie of the Mummel-Lake;" "The Wild Huntsman;" "St. Ursula;" "Lohengrin;" "The Firebell of Cologne;" "The Archbishop's Lion;" "The Magic Banquet;" "The Hunchbacked Musician;" "The Treasure Seeker;" "The Dragon's Rock;" "Stolzenfels: The Alchemist;" "The Dance of Death;" "The Blind Archer;" "The Mouse Tower;" "The Knight and the Yellow Dwarf;" "The Maiden's Leap;" and many more! Journey down the Rhine with Lewis Spence as he shares the legends of the ancient castles and cities found along the shores of this mighty river!

ISBN: 978-1-880954157

Wonder Tales from Baltic Wizards:
Pagan Mythology, Shamanism, and Magic from
Finland, Lapland, Estonia, Latvia, and Lithuania
by Frances Jenkins Olcott

In Lapland, four great wizards join the wizard Nischergurje for a night of storytelling. There is Kauko, Red-Haired Wizard of Finland; Sarvik, with woolly white hair, come from Estonia's rocky coast; yellow-eyed Kurbads from Latvia of the crystal streams; and Jakamas of Lithuania, with bushy golden head, pointed eyes, and apple cheeks. And each wizard carries his own Magic Drum. *Beat! Beat! Beat!*

ISBN: 978-1-880954-16-4

Made in the USA
San Bernardino, CA
30 March 2015